CW00347579

Surrender
TO
YOUR
Adversity

Surrender
TO
YOUR
Adversity

How to Conquer Adversity,
Build Resilience, and Move
Toward Your Life's Purpose

ROB SWYMER

*BOOK*LOGIX˙
Alpharetta, GA

ISBN: 978-1-6653-0319-4 - Hardcover
ISBN: 978-1-6653-0311-8 - Paperback
eISBN: 978-1-6653-0312-5 - eBook

Library of Congress Control Number: 2022900370

Printed in the United States of America   0 1 2 7 2 2

∞ This paper meets the requirements of ANSI/NISO Z39.48-1992 (Permanence of Paper)

*To Missy, for giving me a
second chance at life and love.*

*In loving memory of Bon Bon.
Without you, there is no story.*

contents

foreword

Too often, we find our lives being controlled by our circumstances. It doesn't have to be this way.

In *Surrender to Your Adversity*, Rob tactfully illustrates how your own internal mental-talk track affects every belief you have and every action you take. As Rob says, life will continue to disappoint you, and it will also surprise you. Adversity comes to all of us. It comes in all shapes and sizes, in doses large and small. And it almost never shows up at the time that is particularly convenient or predictable.

From the way you respond to adversity, to your daily habits, to the way you do or don't set goals for yourself, your mindset is the creator of your reality.

By examining his own hard losses (the unexpected death of a beloved partner, substance abuse, and other family challenges), along with the adversities of others, Rob demonstrates that whatever adversities you may encounter, they don't have to be permanent setbacks. While we may not choose our adversities, we are at complete choice about our response to them.

Rob Swymer takes you on a journey to free yourself from the constraints of what's happening around you. He demonstrates how even seemingly large setbacks can be opportunities, that allow us to live more gracious, courageous, and authentic lives.

One of the things I love about this book is that Rob challenges the traditional notion of resilience as a character trait. Instead, he shows us that resilience is a skill that can be learned. For many of us, this comes as welcome relief, because it tells us that our past responses to adversity do not have to define our future responses. It also shows us that resilience, like any other skill, will improve if we continue to practice it over time.

Inside the pages of this book, Rob provides a straightforward path for shifting your mindset and improving your resilience. As he says, if you can change your mindset from the top, the rest of your soul and life will follow.

As you look at your past or current adversities, Rob challenges your thinking, asking you to consider: What if every seemingly negative experience you've had was pointing you toward something bigger. What if inside of every challenge, you could find purpose?

The subtitle of this book is: How to Conquer Adversity, Build Resilience, and Move Toward Your Life's Purpose. There isn't a human being alive who doesn't want more of those skills.

It starts with you and your inner voice. When you decide that you're ready to shift yourself, the whole world takes notice.

Rob has laid out a template. Now it's your turn. Are you willing to dive in?

—Lisa Earle McLeod
Author of *Selling with Noble Purpose* and
Leading with Noble Purpose

introduction

A Letter to the Reader

*Hard times don't create heroes. It is in the hard time
that the "hero" within us is revealed.*

—Bob Riley

How ironic that I decided to write a book about overcoming adversity while I am again overcoming adversity. As I sit here in London working on this book, we are facing unprecedented times, one year into a pandemic that shut down the entire world. No matter your political or scientific views, we are all in this together, learning as we go.

The COVID-19 pandemic and the resulting economic impact have negatively affected many people's mental health and created new barriers for people already suffering from mental illness and substance-abuse disorders. During the pandemic, about four in ten adults in the United States reported symptoms of anxiety or depression.[1] Yet another study, from July 2020, found that many adults are reporting specific negative impacts on their mental health and well-being, such as difficulty sleeping

---

[1] https://www.kff.org.

(36 percent) or eating (32 percent), increases in alcohol consumption or substance use (12 percent), and worsening chronic conditions (12 percent) due to worry and stress over the coronavirus. As the pandemic wears on, ongoing and necessary public health measures expose many people to situations linked to poor mental health outcomes, such as isolation and job loss.[2]

In a recent survey conducted by the Centers for Disease Control and Prevention, 63 percent of eighteen- to twenty-four-year-olds reported symptoms of anxiety or depression, with 25 percent reporting increased substance use to deal with that stress and 25 percent saying they'd seriously considered suicide. Eighty-one thousand and three: that's the number of people who died from drug overdoses in the twelve-month period ending in June 2020. It was a 20 percent increase and the highest number of fatal overdoses ever recorded in the United States in a single year.[3]

In an online survey carried out by New York University, alcohol and drug use among young people is reportedly increasing as youth resort to substances as a coping mechanism. Lead researcher Ariadna Capasso says the pandemic could be triggering an epidemic of substance abuse. These findings seem to be supported by a broad study carried out by the Centers for Disease Control and

[2] Alkhouri, Dana, "Pandemic's Mental Health Burden Heaviest Among Young Adults," February 21, 2021, https://abcnews.go.com/Health/pandemics-mental-health-burden-heaviest-young-adults/story?id=75811308.

[3] Bensaid, Adam, "Covid-19 has Triggered a Silent Pandemic of Depression and Anxiety," February 15, 2021, https://www.trtworld.com/magazine/covid-19-has-triggered-a-silent-pandemic-of-depression-and-anxiety-44191.

Prevention, which analyzed more than 180 million emergency room visits from December 30, 2018, to October 10, 2020, reporting that 2020 saw 45 percent more drug overdoses.[4]

During the COVID-19 pandemic, concerns about mental health and substance use have grown, including concerns about suicidal ideation. In January 2021, 41 percent of adults reported symptoms of anxiety and/or depressive disorder, an estimate that has been largely stable since spring 2020. In a survey from June 2020, 13 percent of adults reported new or increased substance use due to coronavirus-related stress, and 11 percent of adults reported thoughts of suicide in the past thirty days. Suicide rates have long been on the rise and may worsen due to the pandemic. Early 2020 data shows drug overdose deaths were particularly pronounced from March to May 2020, coinciding with the start of pandemic-related lockdowns.[5]

I could write an entire book on these disturbing trends in mental health. What started out as a physical health crisis with high death rates has now led to long-lasting mental health effects. My fear is that, as you read this book, these numbers have increased significantly. Now, more than ever, we need tools that will help us overcome adversity and thrive when all this passes, and it will.

---

[4] Bensaid, Adam, "Covid-19 has Triggered a Silent Pandemic of Depression and Anxiety," February 15, 2021, https://www.trtworld.com/magazine/covid-19-has-triggered-a-silent-pandemic-of-depression-and-anxiety-44191.

[5] Panchal, Nirmita. Kamal, Rabah. Cox, Cynthia. Garfield, Rachel, "The implications of COVID-19 for Mental Health and Substance Use," February 10, 2021, https://www.kff.org/coronavirus-covid-19/issue-brief/the-implications-of-covid-19-for-mental-health-and-substance-use.

I wanted to tell my story of adversity so that maybe someone would connect to it, learn from it, and use the tools I have used to overcome. My story is a very real and true experience, one that many of you might well relate too. I am a guy who happened to have his share of adversity. What sets me apart is that I dug deep to find ways to rise and discover a new purpose in life, no matter how bad things got. That's where the real work is done.

Sometimes it is a comfort to hear from another person who went through and is still going through adversity. It can be especially impactful when it is an ordinary person who suffered and overcame, not a famous athlete or celebrity. It can be hard to relate to the stories of the rich and famous. I wanted to write a book that was based on my ordinary life. I am a survivor of addiction and can tell you firsthand that, at my lowest, it wasn't the celebrity spokesperson or the wealthy businessman who helped me. It was the addict who had the sobriety and the tools I needed to learn who made the difference.

I needed to fully immerse myself in the program and develop a new vision for myself and how I wanted to live without alcohol. It took a lot of work, but it was all worth it. What I soon realized is that we are all on a level playing field when in the grips of addiction. No amount of money or fame matter at that point. You listen to those who have gone through it and walked in your shoes. Recovered addicts are the ones who will get you through it. They are the only ones who can help, because they get it. They get you.

My hope is that you take something from this book and apply it to your life. Maybe just a little of what I went through can help you thrive again. Remember that everyone has a story, and all types and forms of adversity matter. The key is to recognize that even small setbacks can be building blocks to put in the adversity bank for later, when you really need it. Looking back, I realize the many times I was able to save up resilience to help in future struggles.

Whether you are going through adversity now or are concerned about someone in your family who is, you can use the tools in this book to help. If you are a parent, these tools can help you enable your child to build up their resilience muscle to use later in life. Ultimately, this will give them the independence they need and the ability to overcome adversity, which will make them stronger as adults.

I ask you to read this with an open heart and see if you can relate, not only to my story but to the many I have included here. I have highlighted everyday people who went through adversity, overcame it, and built their resilience muscle. Some of those I feature went on to become life coaches, authors, firefighters, mothers, fathers, and, in my eyes, superheroes. My dream is that this book will be your roadmap to finding your inner superhero.

chapter 1

The Night Everything Changed

*Love is a fabric which never fades, no matter how
often it is washed in the water of adversity and grief.*

—Robert Fulghum

I t was a warm Monday afternoon in July. Bonnie had a
few friends over. In the hot Atlanta weather, they were
all cooling off with a dip in the pool. Our pool was always
busy, filled with friends and family members having fun
and hiding from the summer heat. While our friends were
at play, I was in my home office working, as usual. I could
hear the music cutting through the air and an exchange of
jokes, the normal sounds of everyone having fun. I could
also, of course, hear the boisterous laughter of my wife,
Bonnie. Her laugh was endearing and brought a smile to
my face. I looked forward to joining the group soon, right
after my workday wrapped.

Bonnie, always attentive, would regularly come into

my office throughout the day to check on me, usually in her bikini, and with a huge smile on her face. She never left without giving me a soft kiss and even occasionally offered a little flash on the way back to the pool. She was always so playful with me, so sexy. Bonnie was a show-stopper. When she entered a room, everyone stopped what they were doing and paid close attention to her every move. You could not take your eyes off her. She was mesmerizing, a force of nature to both men and women.

After I completed my work for the day, I put on my swimsuit and headed out to the pool to relax and join in on the fun. By then, it was just Bonnie and another couple hanging out around the pool. We were all in the hot tub, planning dinner for that night and discussing our week-end plans. Our house was the place to be, and the party never seemed to stop. The front door was always open, and our friends and family knew they were welcome. They took full advantage of this open invitation, regularly stopping by for a drink or a quick dip in the pool. Bonnie was her happiest when she had people around her. I often said that if it was your first time at the Swymers', you'd feel like family by the time you hit the kitchen and got your welcome hug from Bonnie.

Things progressed as usual at the pool, from beer and wine to cosmopolitan cocktails—one of Bonnie's favorite drinks. At that point in my life, my recovery program was strong, and I could be around people consuming alcohol without any effect on me at all. Not everyone in recovery can do this, but I remain grateful that I could still enjoy my friends and be around a party atmosphere without craving alcohol. The only way this could have happened is through a strong sobriety program and constant resolve.

It was getting late; the setting sun appeared to be a beautiful, bright-red and orange ball in the sky. As I relaxed in the hot tub, I was so grateful for the life Bonnie and I had built together. We worked so hard to get where we were, and we never took it for granted. We always shared our happiness with everyone around us, as that was important to Bonnie.

I still remember the moment it happened, just before seven o'clock. We were all enjoying the hot tub, talking and laughing with one another. I looked over my shoulder to see Bonnie had leaned over the waterfall and was looking into the pool. I thought nothing of it at first, figuring she was splashing some cold water on her face to cool down. But after a short time, I went over to check on her. When I turned her around, I knew something was terribly wrong. She was unresponsive, her eyes closed with little color in her face. I shook her, tapping her face to try and wake her up. I was yelling her name at the top of my lungs, though she was mere inches away from me. I prayed she would wake up, but my cries were met with no response.

Meanwhile, our friend frantically called 911. I kept yelling, "Wake up, wake up." It all seemed like a blur, like everything was moving in slow motion. It was an out of body experience. I sat there, in the hot tub, holding her, still helplessly trying to wake her up. It seemed like my efforts lasted forever.

As you can imagine, I was quickly running out of patience. I had our friend hold Bonnie while I ran out to the front yard to flag down the ambulance. What was taking them so long? I kept running back and forth from the front yard to the pool, inquiring if there was any response from Bonnie. There was nothing. In extreme despair, I could still smell the faint scent of the jasmine she had planted around the pool. Although subtle, the smell ripped through the air as my heightened senses took it all in.

When the ambulance finally showed up, I watched from a distance as the paramedics worked on her by the pool. It seemed to take forever, but they eventually stabilized her enough so they could transport her to the hospital. The ride to the hospital felt long. I kept asking the driver to go faster, confused and still in my out-of-body-experience state. From the front seat of the ambulance, I looked back through the window and saw the paramedics using paddles to revive Bonnie. That image will be etched in my mind until the day I die. I felt hopeless watching a piece of my heart struggle for every breath. I wish that feeling on no one.

It was total chaos when we arrived at the hospital. I ran to the back of the ambulance to tell her I loved her, that I would always be there for her. I wanted to reassure her that I was by her side. Her eyes were still closed, and she showed no response. The paramedics rushed Bonnie into the trauma room, and I followed along until they left me behind in the waiting room.

I sat in total shock, unable to believe this was happening to me, to our family, to my beloved Bonnie. In that cold and weathered waiting room, I rocked in the hard and uncomfortable chair while reciting the Serenity Prayer, repeatedly: "God, grant me the serenity to accept the things I cannot change, the courage to change the things I can, and the wisdom to know the difference." That prayer had saved my life on many previous occasions. In that moment, it was the only thing I could think of to calm my nerves. I recited the prayer over and over again, nervously rocking from side to side and hoping this would soon pass.

Bonnie and I met over thirty-three years before that fateful evening. We had our ups and downs, like any other couple, but we always came out of it stronger, together. We were just about to enter our next chapter as empty nesters; our three children were away at school or on their own. Just days before, we were talking about all the places we wanted to see. In fact, we were planning an upcoming trip to Italy, which was just a few weeks away. We had recently welcomed our first grandchild into the world, and it seemed as if life couldn't get any better. But life clearly had other plans. I couldn't imagine, could not even contemplate, how or why this occurred. As I prayed, I had faith that this was just another test, another life event that would create more resilience. I trusted it wouldn't be an event that left me a broken man.

I was finally able to see Bonnie in the trauma room. As I entered, I expected to see my Bonnie smiling back at me, reassuring me all would be fine, just like she always did when life threw us a curve ball. But that wasn't the case. Instead, as I turned the corner, I noticed tubes, machines, and lots of nurses around her. I quickly realized Bonnie was on life support with a tube in her head, blood draining right out of it. I was confused. *What is going on here?* The nurses saw I had entered the room and immediately tried to calm me down. The doctor eventually came in to tell me Bonnie had suffered a massive brain aneurysm while in the hot tub.

I remained by her side from that moment on. I never left her. The staff worked on her all night, trying different procedures and medicine—anything that might bring her back. By now, word had gotten out to all our friends and neighbors. They flooded the waiting room to cling onto any news they could get. It was just like back at our family pool, everyone stopping by and surrounding us with love. I sent for my children: Nicole in Savannah; Eric in Los Angeles; and Wes in DC. I called Bonnie's mom in Florida and my brother-in-law on Cape Cod to let them know they needed to get to the hospital as quickly as possible.

At one point, I decided to take a quick walk around the ICU. It was then that I noticed that our friends and family remained in the waiting room. They refused to leave. They wanted to be close to Bonnie. The entire waiting room was packed with friends and neighbors. All that love and support was overwhelming. One of my good friends owned a restaurant, and he brought food in for everyone. In true Bonnie fashion, we took over the waiting room.

My kids eventually arrived, along with Bonnie's mom and my brother-in law. By Tuesday, it was becoming clear that our Bonnie was not going to come back; the damage was just too severe. I had Wes, my youngest, update the waiting room while I called extended family to let them know the tragic news. These proved to be some of the most difficult conversations I would ever have in my life. But I had no choice. Repeatedly, I heard disbelief and tears on the other end of the line. I wanted to be the one to call; I wanted them to hear my voice. I needed them to know I was going to be all right and that I was strong and would be there for my kids.

So many came to say good-bye to Bonnie that the staff had to organize and direct the steady flow. So much love yet so much sadness filled these visitors. I will never forget how my middle boy, Eric, sat by his mother's bedside for three days straight, holding her hand and sobbing from the pain of losing his mother. It was tough realizing that my daughter, who had just welcomed her first little one, would have to face being a mom by herself without Bonnie's guidance, love, and support. I thought about the fact that Wes, my youngest child who was only twenty years old at the time, would live a great part of his life without his mother. As a dad, nothing hurts more than seeing your kids suffer yet having no ability to take that suffering away.

It is crazy what goes through your mind as you experience something like this. Bonnie and I were together since we were nineteen. We grew up together. She was the glue of our family, the center of everyone's universe. We had been through so much together, so many ups and downs. I had no idea what was next for me, but I knew God had a plan. In my life, no matter what I faced, I faced it with faith, not fear.

Despite the pain and suffering, I decided in that moment to be a model for my children, my family, and my friends. I wanted to send the message that we were all going to be all right. At that point in my life, I had twenty years of sobriety. My journey to sobriety helped me understand you must hand your fate over to God and accept his plan for you. If I didn't believe in that, I would have left this life a long time ago. I made the decision that I would find our new normal. But as I made that decision, I wasn't sure how it would be possible. I would have to find a new purpose and a new perspective. Only through surrender could I find a way to move forward.

I remember walking through those hospital hallways. Room after room was filled with people clinging on to dear life. I saw family after family standing in the hallway in tears, wondering how they would recover from their pain. Each represented a different story, a special journey, a remarkable loss.

Through my experience with losing a loved one far too soon, I realized we all experience adversity. How you choose to deal with it, however, is your choice. Looking back at my life, I see that I had to make a conscious decision to move forward, learn from the experience, and come out of it with a higher purpose. You will hear me say many times that I believe "life is happening *for* me, not *to* me." In even my darkest hours, this motto has saved me every time.

We made the decision to take Bonnie off life support on July 31, 2013, three days after she suffered that massive brain aneurysm. I laid there next to her, my hand on her chest as she took her last breaths. I felt as her chest rose a little lower each time, slower and slower until there was no more. I studied her face, her lips, her hair, her cheeks; everything about her was like it had been the first time I saw her on our blind date back in college. Knowing this would be the last time, I needed to remember every detail. In the end, I just didn't want to leave her side. My brother-in-law, who I love with all my heart, was by my side the entire time. The hardest thing I had to do was walk out of that room knowing I would never see her in this lifetime again. It was surreal.

Grief can be very unpredictable. A year after Bonnie's passing, I was getting ready to sell our family home. I had to clean out her art studio. Among all the other talents she had, Bonnie was an accomplished artist. As I was going through the studio, I found myself on my knees sobbing, overcome by emotion. Most days, I was in a great place and did a good job of moving forward and going on with life, but these moments reminded me that grief can come and go without any warning. For all those dealing with loss, turn to your faith and know there is a bigger plan that we don't get to control. I am thankful to have so much love around me every day. There is life and love after loss, but that doesn't mean you forget. You don't move on from the person you lose, you move on with that person in your heart forever.

This is not a book about grief so much as it is about what I have experienced in my journey through life so far. I have learned that you don't come into this life with resilience. Rather, it is a muscle you must strengthen. We learn resilience along the way and build up the ability to deal with hardship as we navigate each one. My dad used to say, "Adversity builds character." As a kid, I wasn't sure what he meant. As I sat in the hospital with Bonnie, holding her hand as she took her last breath, that quote rang in my ear. I knew I needed to show character and be strong. I believe that there is nothing I cannot handle if I apply the simple principle of surrendering and moving forward with new purpose and perspective. The adversity I faced in my life as a young child and throughout my adult years created a strong sense of resilience, an ability to cope with life on life's terms. Every challenge in my life had gotten me ready for the moment I told Bonnie good-bye.

My hope is that somewhere between the lines of my story you can take a bit of what I learned and apply it to your life, your challenges, and your ability to live life on life's terms. No matter how big or small the adversity you experience, you can overcome it and thrive again if you learn from it. I acknowledge I am just a guy who went through his share of shit, survived it, came out the other side, and is now thriving more than ever. I have gone from having nothing, bouncing checks to pay for diapers in my younger years, to living my life with the financial freedom I always dreamed of. I like to joke with my kids that it took me sixty years to become an overnight success. It is indeed a lifelong journey.

Ask yourself, what is next for you in this life? I get asked that all the time. My answer is always the same: "I am not really sure, but I know that the universe will bring it to me when I am ready, and I am so excited to see what it is." After all, what could possibly beat me after losing Bonnie?

Here is what I know with 100 percent conviction: Everyone has a story, and every story has some sort of adversity or challenge. The difference is that some people bounce back, continue to move forward, and continue to thrive. Others fall victim to the challenge and can never fully recover. Why do some succeed while some fall short? What is the quality shared by those who succeed? We never stop moving, learning, growing, and loving. We accept the bigger plan and trust the journey. In the end, the difference is that we surrender to move forward.

I met Bart in my late twenties. We worked for a small company together, located outside of Boston. The two of us had an instant connection, becoming very close to one another. As I navigated my career as a sales leader in the software industry, I would always ask Bart to be a part of my team. We worked together at several companies throughout the years. I trusted him with my life, and we worked very well together. Bart was an adrenaline junkie. A Marine sniper in his younger years, when he wasn't selling software, he was heli-skiing or racing cars.

One year, when Bonnie couldn't attend one of my sales incentive trips, I took Bart. We were inseparable. We had genuine love for each other. Every time we spoke or saw one another, our parting words were "I love you, man." I remember when I told Bart that I was in AA and that I was going to be okay. We were having dinner together and he reached across the table and touched my face with his hand. He looked into my eyes and let me know he was there for me and that he had my back. It was hard to leave him behind when I moved to Atlanta with the family, but we stayed close even when we weren't in the same city for work.

Not too long after we moved to Atlanta, I received a call from his fiancée that changed my life forever. She told me that Bart, his dad, and several other friends were returning from a hunting trip in Canada when their charter plane went down. Bart and the others instantly died. The voice on the other line simply said, "He is gone."

This was the first big loss I had in my life. It rocked me. I took the next flight to Boston to be with friends and family. Bart was Jewish, so we took turns spending time with his body at the funeral home until we were able to bury him. The Jewish tradition of shiva requires a week of mourning, and I stayed in Boston the entire time. Time seemed to stand still and there was an unmeasurable amount of grief, a feeling I had not experienced before. I had lost my best friend, my brother from another mother. Although he has now been gone for twenty-five years, I still find myself thinking of him and all the memories that we had together. I still look to the heavens and talk to him and ask for support when I need it. I know he is up there with Bonnie, helping to watch over me and my family.

Everything happens for a reason. I believe that this event ultimately helped prepare me for other loss in my life, like when I lost my father, my mom, and eventually my wife. We are never really ready for loss, and it affects us in different ways depending on who and where you are in life. Loss is a part of life and a part of living. Know that there is a grand plan and that all will be okay. It has taken me a lifetime to get to this place so don't be too hard on yourself. Be open to feeling the emotions and be grateful for the moments you have with loved ones. We don't have the control of when they leave us, but we can control how present we are for them when they are here.

The reality is that it is a top-down solution that starts with your mindset. If you can change your mindset from the top, then the rest of your soul and your life will follow. Superheroes understand that, and so can you. They have all faced adversity and delt with loss or grief, yet superheroes thrive and keep moving forward with a winner's mentality and mindset. They all find new purpose in life and use that purpose to move on and thrive again. They are obsessed with that purpose and make it their life mission. I call this the "superhero mindset," and I believe it is one of my best tips for facing adversity. When life presents heartache, I summon my superpowers and set my mind to overcome. The good news is that we all can become superheroes and thrive. Once you decide you are going to do it, it all comes down to taking action.

My story not only defines the superhero mindset but also outlines in detail the steps you can take to build resilience muscles and thrive after any negative life event. It does not matter the size of the experience or event. This all applies to you. The truth is each experience has varying degrees of impact, but each presents an opportunity to build resilience. The key is to use every life event to get stronger for the next. Life will continue to disappoint and surprise you. You have to be ready to handle what comes your way and to bounce back quicker and stronger each time.

What if our ability to surrender is the key to building resilience and your superhero mindset?

What if giving in is the most important step you can take to move past your challenges?

I ask you to take this journey with me, and you can decide.

chapter 2

Meet Adversity: The Greatest Teacher

Adversity shakes the foundation of our character to see if what we believe and value is really worth standing for.

—Rae Smith

*A*dversity is often an unwelcomed word. But as surely as the sun rises and sets, adversity is going to be a part of your life. It is a common human experience, like waking each morning and going to bed in the evening. It is a given. Even so, most of us do everything we can to avoid adversity, trying our best to tiptoe around it and find less painful paths.

However, adversity has been part of life since day one; it cannot be avoided. To that end, we must learn to accept it and make peace with it. For it is through surrender to adversity that growth occurs. Only through adversity can we build the resilience that will help us survive devastating life events and learn to thrive again.

Adversity: Unwelcomed, Unavoidable, Necessary

We are not born resilient. Rather, we develop resilience as we interact with our environment. Psychology offers us some guidance here, defining supportive relationships with parents, coaches, teachers, caregivers, and other adults in the community as some of the most vital and active ingredients for building resilience. But these relationships alone, while extremely valuable to your growth, will not get you there. It takes so much more, and that is where you come in. Resilience is not a trait; it is a skill that is developed over time through adversity.

Perhaps the most impactful and meaningful way to forge resilience is through a simple yet powerful act: surrender. By *surrender*, I do not mean giving up. Rather, I am referring to the remarkable act of giving *in*. That one word will make all the difference in your journey. My personal experience with surrender has given me the conviction to pass this on to you.

When faced with adversity, the majority of people get stuck in shock or anger, blaming others for where they are and how they feel. However, surrender is the cure to being stuck. This simple act can make so much pain go away. Through surrender, we become humble and willing to learn, to grow, to pivot, and take action. This must be a deliberate, conscious shift. You must want it and then dedicate yourself to working at complete surrender.

One of the toughest days of my life was the day I got on my knees, surrendered, and asked for help in AA. Ultimately, that action not only changed my life but saved it. A simple act of surrender illuminated the otherwise dark path to healing.

I didn't have my first drink until my second year of

college; I just didn't feel the need for it. I was focused on my dream of playing college basketball and wanted to stay focused and remain in good shape. I took care of myself and didn't drink or smoke. But everything changed at my first fraternity party. In the center of the room was a huge keg of beer. "Take a cup and help yourself," one of the older frat brothers suggested to me.

I was not prepared for this at all. The beer gave me a feeling I never had before. I was transformed into someone else: the cool guy. I was popular and confident, able to let loose and party like I had never done before. I didn't want it to end. Unfortunately, it didn't end for a while, but my dreams of being a collegiate athlete eventually did.

Halfway through the season, I noticed I was off my game, not able to perform at my peak. I was drinking a lot, and it was starting to show. I remember trying to get sober before a game after being out all night. I sat in a hot sauna to get the alcohol out of my system, hoping I could be effective enough to play in the game just hours away. I sat there in the sauna wondering what had happened to me. *How did I get here?*

My drinking escalated so quickly that I didn't know what hit me. At one point, I woke up in the morning under a car in the student parking lot, with no recollection of how I ended up there in the first place. Looking back, it was likely another moment where God was looking out for me, preventing a car from running me over. I certainly wasn't worthy of his grace and protection at the time.

Over the course of the next several months, alcohol became my priority. I was still holding on to my grades and keeping up, but everything else just faded away. I eventually lost the ability to play ball at a high level. After my sophomore season came to an end, I gave up on my dream to play on the varsity team. I told myself that I needed to focus on my grades. It is amazing the kind of story you tell yourself to justify floating away in the direction of your choice. Since then, I have learned that if you change your inner voice, you can change your life. My story was that alcohol made me cool, a bigger man, a better person, a more successful individual. I was unbeatable. But in truth, I was living a total lie. I was none of those things. Rather, I was a fake. Have you ever felt that way? If so, what is your story? Are you willing to change it?

Life continued, and I ultimately had a decent college experience, enjoying the fraternity experience and keeping my grades up. I made the dean's list at Bentley a few times and graduated with above-average grades. Who would have thought? The guidance counselors who told me I would never go to college would have been particularly surprised. While I found a way out of college with reasonable success, I had not abandoned my drinking habits. Those would stay with me for years to come.

As it turns out, I still had suffering to endure before I would realize my only solution was to surrender. I masked or drowned my pain for the next fifteen years of my life. While I did enjoy some success during that time period, I found very little fulfillment or purpose. I focused on the wrong priorities and lost a lot of time I'll never get back—time with the kids, with friends, and of course, with Bonnie. Not a day goes by that I don't think about this period. I would do anything to get that time back.

Look at where you are now in life. Who or what do you wish you had more time with? You can make the decision right now to stop wasting your time. One of my favorite quotes from Warren Buffet, one of the richest people in the world is, "I can buy anything I want in life, except more time."[6]

Think of the times in your life you might have experienced a particular challenge. Maybe you were bullied as a kid or didn't feel like you fit in. Were you ever lonely or just frustrated at a situation that was out of your control? That is adversity. It comes in all different shapes and sizes; it can be a tidal wave or a series of small yet powerful waves crashing into you. It can build up in little doses. A failing relationship, a career that is not inspiring, or a friendship that is toxic — these examples of adversity sneak up on you without warning. If you don't open your heart, those learning moments will pass you by. I ask you to keep your heart open to these moments going forward. When you think about giving in, surrender to them so you can move on and grow from them.

I am grateful for the adversity I have experienced and wouldn't trade any of it. I know that statement may seem crazy, but without adversity, I would not be sharing this story with you. Life is happening *for* us, not *to* us. The adversity you are going through now is building your resilience and getting you ready for the challenge that will come your way in the future. Embrace adversity and thank it for being a part of your life. Adversity is not who you are; it's just an outside experience that you need to face, manage, and ideally overcome. The key is to learn and grow each time. It took me a long to time to surrender in my early years, and I paid the price for it.

I knew I had a problem with drinking but continued to deny it. My life was out of control; I was making poor decisions and putting the next drink above providing for my

---

[6] https://www.fool.com/investing/best-warren-buffett-quotes.aspx.

family, above my marriage, and above my health and my life. I would always find the money to buy beer or scotch, but many times, I couldn't even afford to buy diapers for my babies. That's a tough pill to swallow as a loving dad. The disease had cast its spell on me; it had full control of my every action. Our neighbors would sometimes show up with care packages to make sure we had the basics. As embarrassing as it was, I couldn't provide for my family and still didn't surrender. I kept fighting till the end.

The last straw for me came as we approached my youngest son's first birthday party. I had a full keg at the party, with the idea it would be more of a frat party than a child's birthday party. We polished off the keg with our friends, with me carrying the greatest load. I was absolutely wasted at my son's birthday party, embarrassing Bonnie and the rest of the family.

But thankfully, some good came out of it. It was, perhaps, my first lesson in surrender. Instead of continuing to fight my demons, I got up the next day and called AA to find out where the next meeting was. I knew I had to get help. I was finally sick and tired of being sick and tired. I dialed the number for a local AA crisis line and a nice woman answered the call. The next moments of that phone call proved to me that God was present in my life. I call it a God moment.

As it turns out, I have had many of those moments in my life, especially once I opened my heart to receive them. The voice on the other end of the call told me about a meeting starting in one hour, just one hundred yards from my house. I had no excuse now, no way to get out of it, no way to procrastinate anymore. I went to that meeting with Bonnie and picked up my first chip. There, for the first time in my life, I admitted to a room full of strangers that

I was an alcoholic and needed help. I could see a look of relief in Bonnie's eyes as she took a big breath and held my hand tightly, assuring me it would be okay; we would get through this together.

Of course, my journey to sobriety was far from a clear and steady path. I refused to fully surrender, and even though I did not drink and went to meetings as prescribed, I did not work the program or live like I should have. Because of that, my early years of sobriety were very difficult. During the first year of sobriety, while on a business trip in New Jersey, I pulled over on Route 17 in Mahwah and sobbed out loud. Sitting in a diner parking lot, I realized I was in a dark place, struggling to get my life back on track. I felt alone and depressed; I didn't want to go on. I called Bonnie from a pay phone and told her that she and the kids would be better off without me. I told her I had failed her as a husband and the kids as a father. In this moment, I wanted to take my own life, to end it right then and there. That is the definition of giving up.

Poor Bonnie had to hear that struggle over the phone. She had to deal with such desperation on the other end of the line, knowing she could not hold my hand, hug me, hold me, or even help me get out of the dark place. I can only imagine how heartbreaking that was for her. I wish I could take that call back. Unfortunately, that was not the only time I had those feelings.

Throughout that first year of getting sober, I went to this dark place a lot. Bonnie and I were so disconnected that I went the entire first year without touching her, without reaching out to her. She kept giving and giving and sticking by my side the entire time, never giving up on me. I know that without God and faith I could not have come out of it. As I got more sobriety under my belt, I knew it was God's power and the love of a great woman that would ultimately lead me to healing.

Work kept me occupied and gave me a purpose. It kept me moving forward. Bonnie and I coexisted at home but nothing more. I buried myself in my career and put all I had into becoming the best I could be at the office, still neglecting my home life. I was somehow able to focus and execute. I saw success at work and gained momentum in life again. I got my confidence back, recognized a few wins, and felt like I was worthy.

When I got my first-year chip in AA, I saw that I could thrive again without a drink. I learned that alcoholism is a cunning and baffling disease that takes control and never let's go. The only solution is to surrender and give in so you can take action toward a new purpose. Does that sound familiar to you? Have you ever been in the position where you had no choice but to surrender, yet you fought it every single step of the way? If so, you aren't broken. Rather, you are normal.

The Antidote to Adversity

No one wants to experience adversity, but we all do. My hope is that you will identify with my stories and envision yourself in similar situations. The life events that hit you hard and have a large impact on the surface matter but so do the smaller events that shaped your life and beliefs at an early age.

It takes courage to surrender and allow life events to teach you. Courage is not a matter of feeling no fear. Rather, it is acting in the face of fear. In sports, they refer to this as "playing nervous." Courage is the strength to face adversity and destructive habits head on. It takes courage for an addict or alcoholic to overcome his addiction, or for the person abused as a child to heal their deep psychological trauma to become a loving and productive adult. Those who move forward in the face of adversity increase their inner strength. They build resilience and tap into their superhero mindset. Anyone can have the courage and follow through to overcome—if they learn the tools, build the muscle, and practice the steps. This is true no matter how small or big the challenge you face.

As adversity creeps in, you must engage your courage. As you continue in the face of fear, you build your resilience muscle. In a recent newsletter published by The Bounce Back Project, the author cites five key aspects of resilience:

1. Self-awareness
2. Mindfulness
3. Self-care
4. Positive relationships
5. Purpose[7]

I would like to add a sixth aspect to this list: courage—the courage to surrender. We become more resilient by strengthening these six areas. It is like going to the gym. You might start out with light weights, but as you get stronger, you can handle more. The same thing happens with your resilience muscle. You must work at it, even through pain and discomfort. That is where the growth happens. Just as people hire personal trainers to push them to do ten reps when they think they can only do eight, you must have a personal trainer to help you build your

---

[7] Unknown Author, "Resilience," accessed July 18, 2021, https://www.bouncebackproject.org/resilience.

resilience muscle. As Norman Vincent Peel wrote, "People don't understand the power of problems. Problems are a sign of life. They build our spiritual muscles, just like the gym. They are the gym for our souls."[8]

This comes in many forms, like asking for help, accepting your place in life, and recognizing a new purpose and perspective. Similar to living life on life's terms, if you embrace the challenge when shit happens, you will find yourself stronger than you originally thought you were. That is where the real growth happens. It is not the first ten reps you do in the gym that count; it is the last three as you near failure and have to push yourself. That is the impact. When you realize the weight isn't impossible to lift or you can actually run the marathon, the magic happens. It all comes down to mindset—the superhero mindset.

Building Your Resilience Muscles

Let's consider each of these six aspects of resilience and apply them to your life.

Self-awareness. Self-awareness is the conscious knowledge of your own character and feelings and is the first step toward resilience. With self-awareness, you can admit where you are and, more important, who you are. This process is a life journey and one that is always changing. When I was younger and dealing with learning disabilities, I had to accept that I had to adapt to find a way to learn. When I entered AA, I needed to admit I had a problem before having any hope of moving forward. You must have the awareness to understand what makes you tick. What are the keys that enable you to pivot, grow, and thrive again?

---

[8] Croxton, Sean, "Episode 103: Quote of the Day Show," March 21st, 2017.

Mindfulness. Mindfulness is the mental state achieved by focusing your awareness on the present moment. When you are building resilience, you have to stay present. I have a saying: "Being present is the best gift you can give." Anxiety takes us far into the future and constructs a negative story of what could happen. Depression makes us wallow in the past. But in the present, you can manifest the amazing life you want, the beautiful state you want to live in.

Self-care. Taking action to preserve or improve your own health is called self-care. Many associate self-care with exercise, massages, or healthy eating. But self-care is also about developing a support network to lean on. You need others who make you feel safe around you in times of need. For some, getting help includes therapy; others lean on friends and family for strength. Either way, when adversity is extreme, you need to seek help to care for yourself. For me, self-care included my family, friends, and of course, the AA fellowship. When adversity is strong, you cannot solve the issues alone.

Positive relationships. Positive relationships are filled with mutual respect, kindness, and empathy. Growing up, I was close to my parents, especially my dad. We had a special bond. He was a charming guy, loved by many. He worked hard for everything he had and moved up the corporate ladder from the bottom. For as long as I can remember, he was in a battle with cancer. He first got cancer during the war when he was in the navy. His life jacket burst, and the chemicals got into his blood stream, causing many issues. Cancer was one of those health-related concerns. He ended up taking early retirement. By the time I was in my early teens, he was on full disability. I got to spend a lot of time with him, and we became very close.

It was during that time that I realized just what he was dealing with when it came to my mom. I point this out now because, although this was not a positive relationship, it impacted my life. She was a very strong woman and always needed to be in control. As I got older and had a family of my own, it became more and more difficult to be around her. I realized later in my life that Dad had shielded me from a lot of her issues. Yet Mom influenced every aspect of my life, from the way I dressed, to the friends I had, to the dreams I pursued.

Dad never complained; he just kept fighting. He fought all the way to the end and finally lost his battle with cancer when I was forty. I miss him every day. He was my role model and a beacon for me when it came to overcoming adversity and building resilience. He went through so much and never gave up. "Big Jim" is missed still, today, and his words and sayings will stay with me forever.

Purpose. Purpose is a person's sense of resolve or determination. When we define our purpose, we firmly decide on a course of action and move forward. Finding your new purpose after adversity is not easy, but without purpose, you will falter and may fall back into a dark place. Purpose gives us the resolve to move forward, to build resilience, and to thrive again. When I lost Bonnie, my new purpose was to be there for my kids, to model moving forward for my family and friends. I took action to move on with Bonnie in my heart.

Courage. Courage is not allowing fear to stop you from taking action. As I write this book in 2020, during a worldwide pandemic, many are facing a choice: live in fear or face the fear and keep living, trusting this, too, shall pass. Those who are courageous will allow this trying time to build resilience. They will not just return to the new normal but will accelerate past it and thrive even more after the virus is gone.

I cannot stress enough that you cannot develop any of these elements alone. Learning to lean on others is part of surrendering. Accepting help is a liberating feeling; you will sense a huge weight lifted off your heart as you heal, take action, and move forward.

The Results of Resilience

In building resilience, it's important to celebrate the little wins. I knew that if I focused on my small improvements, I could keep moving forward. Have you ever been on a diet or started an exercise program? Why do people weigh themselves each and every day? They want that little win they feel when seeing a pound or two go. The amount doesn't matter as long as they can feel progress.

As you celebrate those little wins, you build momentum. The small changes eventually turn into massive shifts. Momentum is the purposeful movement toward a goal, a vision, or a desired destination. In many ways, there is no better feeling. So how do we build momentum when dealing with adversity? A key word is *purposeful*. We must define our desired destination, the better life we are striving for.

In the end, it all comes down to mindset: the superhero mindset. Having a superhero mindset means doing whatever it takes to be prepared. Remember, superheroes don't just survive. They overcome and thrive. We all can change our mindset anytime we want. As I said before, it is a top-down solution that starts between your ears. You have to decide and then take action to apply that mindset.

It doesn't matter your life stage; you can tap into your

superhero mindset and change where you are going at any point in time. We have a saying in AA: "I am sick and tired of being sick and tired." When the pain is great enough and your current state is dark enough, you have to call on your superhero mindset to move forward and take action. Here is an example from my friend, Gaelle Lebray.

As Gaelle Lebray approached her fortieth birthday, the stockbroker and amateur triathlon champion found her relationship in shambles and her exhausting career in need of a pivot. She wasn't sleeping anymore and was crying all the time. Gaelle was obsessed with fixing this relationship. She was willing to do whatever it took to change it, as she could not accept the current situation. She began a spiritual journey that led her to a "year of transformation," which culminated in a career shift into coaching.

Gaelle was desperately searching the internet for how to fix her relationship, watching video after video, reading books and online articles. Each time she thought she had identified what the problem was, it was never enough. She became like an addict searching for the next fix. She even started attending self-development seminars, taking full responsibility for what was happening. She remembers this period of searching: "Clearly it was my fault. I didn't know how to communicate. I was not listening. I was jealous. I was a people pleaser." Though she couldn't fully identify the root issue, the suffering was real.

One Friday afternoon, Gaelle was talking to a girlfriend, and like many times before, she was in tears. Her friend told her she could not carry on like this. But Gaelle felt she couldn't leave and said, "I have way too many responsibilities. You know I am the breadwinner."

The next morning, she went for a bike ride, and when she came back, she looked at herself in the mirror. She remembers this moment: "I literally stopped in my tracks and tears flowed down my cheeks. I looked exactly like my grandma when she passed away two years before. The difference was, she was eighty-five." Gaelle was half that age. That was it. It was time to take massive action toward a new purpose. In that moment, Gaelle called on her su-perhero mindset.

She realized that she had to become the most important person again. She sat down with her partner and ended it. As she walked away from the expectation of a dream life, she slept again, felt lighter, and stopped crying. The stress disappeared slowly. Her nervous system calmed down as she was no longer in a state of constant fight or flight. She was living again. Gaelle had finally surrendered so she could move forward. Leaving was the action she needed to take to change her life entirely. This, alongside attend-ing personal-development seminars, put Gaelle on the right track. A focus on self-care and a willingness to reach out for help enabled her to thrive again.

One thing that came out of this deep inner work was a massive certainty; Gaelle felt it was her purpose to help others. She had an unshakeable belief that it was her turn to support those who felt stuck and unsure. Now, Gaelle is an international Life Beyond Heartbreak coach, co-author, and speaker who empowers others to start their own journeys of self-discovery and healing. She also be-lieves that getting out of herself and helping others was one of the most important things she did on her own jour-ney back from adversity.

Gaelle knows from experience that leaving an unhealthy relationship can open the door to new opportunities, in-cluding being ready to attract the perfect partner when the time is right. "All our experiences are lessons, and not seeing it this way is missing the opportunity to step into our full potential," she said. She challenges us all by saying, "Now, would you go on a trip with your old luggage full of your dirty old clothes from your last trip? How would you feel if you were jumping into a new relationship with all your old luggage? How might that impact your new partner you are starting to date? What do you think would happen after a while? Life beyond divorce, beyond separation, beyond heartbreak is rewarding once you learn to have a great relationship with yourself and get rid of the unnecessary baggage. Look at the opportunity as if you have a second chance to live your life on your own terms, reinvent yourself, and chase those personal dreams."

It takes courage to manifest a superhero mindset and forge ahead through adversity. As you strengthen your resilience muscle, you will cultivate the ability to overcome anything that comes your way. Surrender is key. The simple act of accepting that which you cannot control is often the bravest step you can take in your journey. Trusting the process and accepting the outcome is hard for most but will inevitably be the impetus to help you reach your greatest dreams and fulfillment.

chapter 3

Adversity and Me: The Gut-Wrenching True Story of Adversity in My Life

It is your reaction to adversity, not the adversity itself, that determines how your life's story will develop.

—Dieter F. Uchtdorf

I have lived a life of adversity. Fighting through substance abuse and losing my wife unexpectedly are the two most obvious examples of how I've faced life's greatest challenges. In each opportunity—yes, I call them opportunities—I learned a great deal, transformed into a stronger man, and recognized how to best navigate unexpected, unwelcomed, and challenging times. The same is likely true for you. We have all experienced, on some level, the pain and suffering that adversity often introduces into our lives. In many ways, it is the tie that binds.

This chapter is about my journey through gut-wrenching adversity. It highlights and focuses on overcoming substance abuse and dealing with the loss of life. As I endured these tragic scenarios, I learned how to navigate pain and suffering. But it all started with my ability to surrender to the journey. It wasn't easy. In fact, it was mostly painful. But only once I let go could I finally get through.

I learned to be an expert in adversity the hard way — through a trial by fire. We will all experience adversity. It is a normal and natural part of life. And it's not just the big life events that have a lasting impact. Rather, adversity can chip away at you, day by day, instance by instance, until you are left bare and beaten. We should look at the little bumps in the road as challenges that add up over time. Small frustrations present lessons we need to learn as well. In some ways, the small stuff is the most dangerous because you don't immediately recognize the peril until it is too late.

I have already detailed the two most impactful events in my life, but I also learned from my experiences in early life. When I was in my early twenties, I was playing peek-a-boo with my two-year-old daughter on the floor of our apartment. While playing, I noticed that things got a bit blurry when I closed my left eye. Up to that point, I never really thought about my eyesight. In fact, growing up, I had an uncanny gift with depth perception, which allowed me to excel as an outside shooter in basketball. So, I noticed the problem but shook it off and figured it was nothing of importance.

As time went on, I continued to notice some issues, especially when I was driving at night. Bonnie became concerned and encouraged me to see a doctor to investigate the problem. For the first time in my life, I went to see an eye doctor. During my examination, he told me that I had something called keratoconus, an eye condition in which the normally round, dome-shaped, and clear window of the eye (cornea) progressively thins, causing a cone-like bulge to develop. This eventually impairs the ability of the eye to focus properly. In my case, over the course of just a few years, this would lead me to become legally blind.

It was quite a shock to experience this, especially being a traveling salesman going from one customer to the next in my car. The threat of losing my license was stressful. I had always been healthy and strong, and now this? Sadly—like I always did—I leaned on alcohol to resolve my conflict. I have played golf since I was nine, so that was another difficult situation to navigate. When things got really bad with my eyesight, my buddies lined me up on the course and pointed in the direction to hit the ball. It should be noted that I know they sometimes pointed me off the mark to get the upper hand. Afterall, what are friends for?

Over the course of the next year, I went to the eye doctor every month to get new glasses and keep track of the acceleration of the disease. I was eventually put on the transplant list and waited as they searched for a donor. I eagerly waited for my chance, hoping I would soon get a new set of headlights to experience the world around me.

But it gets a bit more complicated. Stick with me here, as you cannot make this stuff up. We all have these stories that seem so painful. But until you write them down and see them on paper, it is hard to accept that all this happened—yet you were able to survive and thrive again. This may not be your story, but I'm sure you have one just like it that allows you to relate. It is all about moving forward and finding a way to thrive again, even when you face adversity in waves, like I did during this time.

Bonnie was pregnant with our second child while I was

struggling with losing my eyesight. I didn't have much time to focus on my own issues since we had a two-year-old at home and were preparing to welcome a new child into the world any day. One evening, Bonnie was making her famous red sauce in advance for our friends' visit in a few days. She made the best red sauce you can imagine, everything from scratch, with special attention to the details. Perfect and plump tomatoes, paper-thin garlic—which she practically shaved apart—and fresh basil were distributed throughout the sauce.

I can almost smell it, deep red with spices, and whatever meat was left over in the fridge. It would come out a little different each time, and every time I would say to her, "This is the best batch you have ever made." She loved it when I said that to her and would return the compliment with that big smile and a huge hug of gratitude. She loved being in the kitchen and serving others. I remember one of my friends getting wind that she had a batch on the stove, and he showed up all the way from New Hampshire just to have a taste. It was that good.

While cooking, she was having labor pains. In between stirring the sauce, we kept track of the contractions to determine if we should rush to the hospital. When they were close enough, we alerted the doctor that we were on the way to welcome our new baby into the world. As we pulled up to the entrance, I remember being so nervous that I left Bonnie in the car and ran to the door without her—not a great move since this wasn't my first experience. Anyway, I caught myself, and ran back to her, opened the car door, and escorted her to the maternity ward.

Labor was extremely long and painful for this one. They tried everything to get this baby delivered. At one point they had her almost upside down on the bed to help induce labor. The next morning, Eric finally arrived. Within seconds the entire medical staff knew something was wrong. They rushed him off to the other room before Bonnie or I could even hold him. The look on Bonnie's face said it all; something was horribly wrong here. The doctor told me to stay with Mom and he would be back in a moment. That moment seemed to take forever.

When he finally did return, he told us that Eric was born with a malrotation of the bowel that occurred late in the pregnancy (around nine days before delivery). His intestine had failed to coil into the proper position in the abdomen and burst. His organs had been burned as a result. They could not locate one of his kidneys and suspected his liver was severely damaged.

They called a trauma medical team from Mass General in Boston to examine Eric and come up with a plan to save his life. I remember holding Bonnie's hand as they brought Eric into the hospital room in the incubator. He was a little over three pounds at birth, and they had inserted tubes in him; his arms and legs were curled up. The only connection we could make with him was to hold his tiny hand through a small hole in the incubator and tell him that we loved him.

We named him Eric. They gave us a polaroid picture of Eric and explained that they needed to get him to Boston so they could further assess the damage. They would report back as soon as they knew what to do. They tempered our expectations, explaining that Eric may not make the forty-five-mile trip to Boston, but they promised to do everything they could to help him.

Another God moment came my way that day as I looked across the room and saw the look on the face of one of the nurses staring back at me from over her surgical mask. Her eyes were familiar, but I couldn't place her. Then she lowered her mask, and I was able to see her entire face. She was my friend from high school. She hugged me and Bonnie to reassure us that they had the best team on the job. They were going to figure this out.

By now, you know a bit about Bonnie. So, I am sure it comes as no surprise that she did not stay in that hospital bed for too much longer before making the trek to Boston to be with her son. We were getting ready to leave when the surgeon from Boston called to let us know that Eric survived the trip. He needed our permission to do exploratory surgery so they could see what they were dealing with. We gave them permission and were on our way.

We arrived at Mass General and were escorted to the prenatal intensive care unit (PICU). There, for the first time, we got to take a good look at him and touch him again through the tiny holes in the incubator. Tubes were everywhere, and machines surrounded him. It was a lot to take in, and for the two of us, only in our early twenties, it was overwhelming.

But picture the scene from *The Grinch Who Stole Christmas*, when the Grinch taps into his superpowers and becomes a force, a true superhero. Bonnie tapped into her superhero mindset and sprung into superhero mode. She asked question after question, trying to get to the bottom of what happened.

It turns out that Eric did have all his organs but had sustained major burns to his insides. They had him on an ileostomy until they could go back in and reverse it a few months later. It was at this point that we noticed casts on his arms and legs, like they were broken. We asked the nurses why he was covered in casts, and they told us the orthopedic team would be up shortly to explain. As if the malrotation was not enough, Eric was also born with arthrogryposis, a very rare birth defect that effects one in five million newborns in the United States. Arthrogryposis describes congenital joint contracture in two or more areas of the body. It derives its name from a Greek word meaning "curving of joints." It is not a term you want to experience. In this case, it severely affected both of Eric's arms and both legs.

We were not prepared for what was next. Eric continued to fight for his life and recover. Some moments, we did not think he would make it. During the first few weeks of life, Eric was given his last rites three times. It was one of the most difficult periods of our life together. However, it brought us closer as we banded together to get through the days and long nights of his recovery.

Eric was in the hospital for a few months, recovering from surgery and getting new casts put on this legs and arms. It became obvious that he would face challenges when it came to his mobility. In fact, it would take thirteen separate operations over the span of five long years, along with daily physical therapy, just to get him to walk. But Bonnie never wavered in her conviction that he *would* walk.

You could say that I had a great role model on how to overcome adversity and build resilience in Bonnie. Watching her orchestrate a team of over twenty doctors and keep track of all Eric's medications, appointments, and progress was like watching a symphony in action. It is because of her that Eric is living on his own today, walking and thriving in Los Angeles. He is an animator and works on some of the top box-office movies we all enjoy.

As if that is not enough, he and his business partner are

running the very first cloud-based virtual animation studio, writing, directing, and producing their first short film. He is a true inspiration to me and to all who meet him. I believe God brought Eric to us for a reason. He has taught me humility, patience, and most of all, how to survive adversity and thrive again. His life has been another God moment to open my heart and cause me to learn.

As with all of my stories of adversity, I reached a point of surrender. During one of Eric's many visits to Mass General, I was walking the halls of the hospital in the middle of the night. I wandered into the chapel. It was then that I surrendered to my higher power and left Eric in his hands. It was truly the moment that defined my ability to let go and have faith rather than fear. This mindset is what has gotten me to this point in my life right now. It all comes down to my sixth element of building resilience: the courage to surrender. The ability to surrender is something I call on often in life as I face other forms of adversity that stand in my path.

So, Bonnie brought home a baby with major medical complications. But wait, there's more. I was also on the wait list for my cornea transplant and still hoping to receive the call before I was unable to drive. Nowadays, this type of procedure is a day surgery with no extended waitlist. Back then, a transplant was a bit more complicated, so it took some time to get the call. We were on the Cape for Thanksgiving when the doctor called to say they had a donor. I was to report to the hospital the next morning for the operation. The timing could not have been better since I was just a few months away from having to renew my license and was in jeopardy of not being able to drive and provide for my family.

We got ready for the surgery and planned to get back

home and to the hospital. Usually, the transplant would be an outpatient procedure, but I would have to be put to sleep and stay overnight. Because I was born with Tourette syndrome, I could not control my movement on the operating table, and it was too risky to keep me awake during the procedure. Even though I had a minor case, it would still manifest itself in uncontrollable movements that the doctor could not risk.

So, there we were, Eric and I, at home recovering together: the old man and his baby. Sounds like a good modern-day play. I don't know how she did it, but Bonnie took care of both of us like a pro. I was able to get back on my feet again in a few weeks and fully recovered within a few months of surgery. I did so with perfect vision, and I was back on track. Onward and upward, I felt ready for the next challenge in life. You see, I know now that all this adversity occurred for a reason. All this adversity prepared me for my future.

Believe in all your heart that no matter what life throws at you, you will face it head on. You will move forward, and you will thrive again. I didn't realize what all this meant when I was going through these times in my life. This wisdom comes with time; if you work on yourself, you may realize just how it all fits together. I share my stories with you not to prove a point but to make a statement: if I can do it, so can you.

The Pain of Struggle

Life quickly improved. Eric was clearly on the path to a better life, and I had perfect 20/20 vision. But sometimes you exchange some adversity for more adversity, and my drinking habits were starting to catch up with me. While we survived these challenging experiences, I never fully surrendered to the pain and the suffering. Rather, I numbed it with excessive drinking. You see, surrender is not just about giving in. Rather, it is about *fully* giving in. I wasn't doing that. I was treating my pain with alcohol. But it wasn't by choice; I was an addict and often reverted to my alcoholic ways to "solve" my problems.

Remember, my journey with alcohol started in college. Even then, I tried to balance grades and, for a while, sports, while living the party lifestyle. From the beginning of my addiction, I fooled myself about its true power by keeping up appearances.

When I met Bonnie the end of my sophomore year, it was love at first sight. I remember the feeling I had when I first laid eyes on her. I knew I was in trouble, and that I had just met the woman I was going to marry. It really does happen like that. I am proof. We saw one another every night after our first date and were married a year later, in between my junior and senior years. I still enjoyed the occasional bender with my fraternity brothers or friends on the weekends. In reality, I was drinking most nights, but we were young and enjoying life. I saw nothing to be alarmed about.

I was what you call a "functioning alcoholic." Even though I was drinking on a regular basis, I could still complete my basic responsibilities: going to school, getting decent grades, and handling life in general. But you know how this story goes. In a little over a decade, I would come to realize I could not lead this double life. Have you ever felt that way? Take a moment to evaluate where you are in life. If you identify with this story, please think about reaching out, getting help, or talking with someone. We have a saying in AA that even though the elevator goes to the basement, you can get off at any floor. This is the time for you to surrender and give in and tap into your super-hero mindset.

Life went on, but my drinking got even worse. I made bad decisions and found myself in the wrong place at the wrong time. On a few occasions, I would say that I relied on a God moment to help me, even though I really didn't know what that was back then. Drinking and partying became a priority. I graduated college, found a sales job, and got the opportunity to hit the road. The drinking joined me while I was away. I could always find an excuse to drink: my favorite team won, my favorite team lost, I made a sale, I lost a sale.

It really didn't matter. Bonnie didn't challenge me much back then, and I was good at hiding the binges from her. I would do my real heavy drinking on the road while traveling for work. With no cell phones back then, I would check in with her and the kids and say good night. As soon as I hung up the phone, I was gone, out for the night to drink with my friends in New York or whatever city I was in.

I told myself that I needed to drink to close the sale; I had to take clients out to have fun to build those relationships. That was the story I kept telling myself. It made sense to me at the time. Even through all the challenges we faced with Eric and my eyesight, I continued to focus on my drinking rather than my family.

One memory stands out. I remember Eric had just gone through another surgery, and I left as soon as he was out of recovery to go to New York on a business trip. The story I told myself was that I had to provide, to make a living, to support my family. I could not wait to get out of there and hit the bars. I couldn't wait to escape my responsibilities and get drunk so I could forget about the pain I was going through inside. I was legally blind at the time, had a physically challenged baby, massive medical bills, and a house that was losing equity every day due to a bad investment. I was just starting out in sales, so I wasn't making a lot of money either. Luckily, I was on an expense account in New York, so I could drink away my lunches and dinners without having to answer to anyone about it.

My career finally did take off, and I became successful at an early age. I was vice president of sales for a small software company by the time I was twenty-seven. Life was moving fast, and I was happy to hold on for the ride. Still able to function and excel at my job, I was the poster child for a functioning alcoholic. I made a decent living over the next few years but not without challenges. We lost our house during this time and had to file for bankruptcy. Even though I enjoyed some success, the medical bills for Eric were just too much to keep up with—or that is the story I told myself. Was that the real reason we lost our house, or was drinking such a priority that I could not thrive at the level of my potential?

After losing the house, we moved into a rental just outside of Boston to start over. We lost just about everything. We were able to keep the car, but during the bankruptcy hearing, the judge took the wedding rings and diamond right off Bonnie's hand. A wave of defeat hit me, seeing the look on her face. She wept in my arms as I held her. It was also during the time that Bonnie gave birth to our third child, Wesley. A year later, I would get drunk for the last time. His first birthday was the turning point for me. With so much pain, my only option was to surrender, give in, and get help.

I mark the moment I stepped into my first AA meeting

back in 1993 as the moment I decided to change my story, to make a change. The story we tell ourselves is what we believe. If you want to overcome adversity and move on with purpose, you should work to change your inner voice. I cannot help but wonder: if I had the tools to make the change sooner, would I have gone through as much pain and suffering? I might not ever be able to answer that question, but I can tell you that timing is everything. You might feel the same way.

How do you change your inner voice? We do this through a conscious decision to stop lying to ourselves. Only the addict can make this choice. We can spend money on therapy and check into the best rehab facility, but if we are not honest with ourselves, it will never work. As the saying goes, change your inner voice, change your life.

I have been sober for close to thirty years now, and I can tell you from experience that my life without alcohol is truly a gift. My first year was a bit rocky, but through being honest, becoming humble, and surrendering, I made progress. Even though I still faced adversity, I could handle it sober.

Besides marrying Bonnie, AA is, without a doubt, the best decision I have ever made. I learned to focus on what I could control. I became a student of AA and live the principles today, staying sober one day at a time.

The Pain of Loss

I had a painful journey to my first AA meeting, but the pain of my early adult years paled in comparison to what my future held. We have all lost someone we love; no one is spared from this painful experience. What does it feel like? It is difficult to describe deep loss adequately. You feel nothing at the beginning. You are numb—or confused, as I was. If you have ever experienced loss, you know exactly what I mean. People always say, "When I lost my loved one, it felt like a piece of my heart died too." But if that is not enough, it also seems like a piece of your "life" dies as well.

When you are with someone, as I was since the age of nineteen, it's the only life you really know. It is hard to remember life without the presence of that person. Bonnie and I grew up together; we experienced hardship and disagreements but came out the other side even stronger. When you lose someone like that, it feels like your world has just stopped. You have nowhere to go, no purpose, no direction. You might find yourself in a state of utter defeat, with no real solution or hope for the future.

When our family and friends returned to their lives after the memorial, a feeling of emptiness settled in. I remember telling myself that I would be okay. I decided to focus on my kids and grandchild; I tried to believe that I didn't need anything else. I felt like I was ready to settle, to accept that I would be alone, that I would never find love again. Pain would be normal, and I would suffer in silence. I didn't know it at the time, but that is not the story you want to tell yourself. Remember, change your inner voice, change your life.

So, I coped by focusing on my family and friends, telling myself I needed to show them that I was going to be okay, that we were all going to be okay. A few months before Bonnie's passing, I had started a job at a software company in Silicon Valley. I immersed myself in my job and focused on getting back in the game. I found a home there, and my work family helped me get through the trauma.

They looked out for me, gave me the time I needed to

grieve, and made sure I had everything I needed to get back on my feet. With their help, I went to grief counseling right away, which helped accelerate the process of healing. I still work at this company today and have formed some of the closest relationships of my life there. I am forever grateful for what they did for me.

In fact, I experienced yet another God moment through my work with this company. I met Marva when she joined the company shortly after Bonnie had passed. She is a fiery redhead who reminded me of Bonnie in so many ways, pint-sized with a personality that is bigger than life. She loves her shoes like Bonnie and loves being around people and connecting. When we met, I was still raw with grief, but I needed a new purpose. As I look back, I believe she was my guardian angel, put in my life to give me the support and care I needed. We still work together, and I have love in my heart for Marva that I will carry for the rest of my life. Marva is one of my most treasured God moments. Today, Marva still drives me to be the best version of myself and to give back to others.

One of the biggest ways I coped with the loss was to get out of myself and think of others. I focused on local charities and found ways to contribute. When you are giving, you are living. The great part about a life focused on giving is that you don't have time to wallow in self-pity. You realize that everyone has a story, everyone has adversity they are dealing with.

What steps can you take to put the pieces back together? I learned later that during one of Bonnie's pool days with her friends just a few weeks before her death, Bonnie had made them promise that if something ever happened to her that they would make sure I didn't go back to drinking. Another God moment? You decide. I stayed focused on what I wanted to model for my children. I didn't fail. I didn't turn to alcohol. I made sure to stay diligent in AA and keep on the right track. It never even crossed my mind to start drinking again. I could never do that to her; she was the reason I was sober all those years.

For me, there was no option but to stay sober and live in tribute to her and all she did for me while she was alive. I also gave myself permission to live again, not to move on from Bonnie, but to move on *with* her. Though it has been several years since she passed, not a day goes by that I don't think of her. She will be a part of my life and in my heart forever. You should give yourself permission to live and find a new purpose. By doing so, I saw a shift from deep sadness to brightening hope.

Through surrender, I acknowledged a bigger plan over which I had no control over. I gave in to the belief that Bonnie was in a better place. I never gave up; I gave in. Fighting with grief is not a good idea as it leads to anger and resentment. On the other hand, when you surrender to it, you accept it, and you manage your expectations. You welcome your emotions and are grateful for them when they come. Be grateful for those emotions and take the opportunity to remember, enjoy, and experience them. The times when a song plays that reminds me of Bonnie or I see her expressions in my children are gifts I cherish.

The Reality of Adversity

Adversity and pain aren't easy to digest. But they are an integral part of life. For example, consider my friend Jobany. At fifteen, Jobany was already planning his future and visualizing what life would eventually look like. He was ambitious with dreams of being successful in America as an immigrant child from Mexico. At seventeen, he studied real estate with hopes of being able to invest someday as a real-life real estate tycoon. One night, his life changed with the ring of the telephone. The authorities notified his mother that there was a past felony on her record and that she needed to report and settle the matter immediately. His mother ended up losing her job and the ability to support her family. Then Jobany's father decided to leave the family and go back to Mexico, leaving Jobany, his brother, and his mom to fend for themselves. Jobany took on the role of caregiver and worked two jobs to support his family. Within two weeks, his life had changed forever.

It ultimately took six months for his mom to clear up all her legal issues. With the little money he had, Jobany began to trade in the stock market. He gave all his money to a friend to invest for him, and she ran away with it, leaving him dead broke. Depression set in, and he began to abuse alcohol and drugs. During this time, he went back and forth to Mexico, trying to find himself in the process. In 2018, he came back to the United States and continued to abuse drugs and alcohol. His brother let him move in with him so he could get back on his feet, but that did not last long. His brother kicked him out due to his reckless behavior and drug use. Jobany moved in with a friend who revealed himself to be part of the drug culture. At one point during the night, Jobany heard the cock of a gun by his head. It turns out that his friend was trying to kill him. He fled that situation and ended up in California.

Throughout his life, Jobany struggled with depression and at one point was suicidal. But, deep down, he always managed to gather enough strength to persevere and come out of it with new purpose. He was able to get a job in California and thrive again. Then the pandemic hit, and he found himself feeling depressed. This is where he found surrender. He learned to think differently. He looked at his obstacles as opportunities to learn and grow. Jobany focused on his dreams and stayed true to the vision he had for his life. He got stronger, hired a personal mentor to help him regain his confidence, and built back his life. Jobany kicked his drug and alcohol habit and reached out to others. He made self-care a priority. Jobany lived in faith, not fear, and joined a church. He put aside one to two hours a day to reflect and focus on self-care, reading, meditating, and working on himself. He found a higher purpose.

His life now is about giving and living for others. Jobany has launched a virtual playground for kids to learn life skills, build confidence, and learn manners through music, dance, and exercise. He has learned that life happens for him and not to him. Through moments of deep reflection, he has been able to connect the dots as to why certain things have happened to make him the person he is today. He believes that what doesn't kill you will only make you stronger, and sometimes the rocks people throw at you will become the hard foundation you need to build upon. In my humble opinion, Jobany is a remarkable example of always remaining dedicated to growth and development.

In the business world, we talk about the importance of having a growth mindset. This is also crucial for your personal life. The principles of a growth mindset include continuous learning, continuous improvement, and becoming comfortable with being uncomfortable. This concept also applies to building resilience. Adversity comes in all shapes and sizes and flavors, but always presents opportunity. That is a key word: *opportunity*. We can find the opportunity for growth in challenging yet fateful moments.

I have described my own personal experiences in adversity. I am no stranger to it. I realize not everyone has lost a spouse, struggled with addiction, or faced blindness. But that doesn't mean you aren't struggling or facing challenges of your own. Everyone goes through adversity.

But how you learn from each event is up to you; it depends on your mindset. If you look at your trial from the lens of a growth mindset, you will continuously learn. No matter how big or small the event, you will use it as a learning experience. You will allow it to change your outlook or behavior as you pivot and adapt so that you can build resilience. Maybe you have lost your job or are struggling with a relationship or have family misunderstandings. A growth mindset is grateful for adversity, no matter how small, and celebrates the day you overcome it. This approach will help you build the momentum that will carry you to the next event and make you even stronger.

Next, a growth mindset focuses on continuous improvement. This is different from learning. This is the act of immersing yourself in personal development. For me, this journey began the moment I met Tony Robbins and applied his principles to my life, both personally and professionally. I realized I had the power to change my outlook, change my story, and thrive again. Whomever your mentor is, make it a mission to develop and dedicate yourself to the cause of personal development. When you do so, you will have purpose and develop a new perspective. All those who have overcome adversity have embraced personal learning and dedicated themselves to living a life of growing.

Lastly, a growth mindset requires the ability to be comfortable being uncomfortable. For example, when working on yourself through therapy or stretching your goals to a new level, you can feel worse before you feel better. You are working through pain and pushing yourself, so it isn't always pleasant. For me, I am always striving to reach that next level. I ask myself, *What can I do today that is different, that will give me an edge?*

Once I changed my mindset, I realized that I could thrive. I had conviction and purpose. That is the life I lead now, a life with no limits and no boundaries. It all started with my mindset and, of course, my ability to surrender. My advice to you is to stop fighting and start living. You have all the power you need inside you to get this done. Everyone has to choose their own journey to a fulfilling life. Choose to surrender, give in, and thrive again. In the next chapter, we will map out the steps needed to accomplish this.

chapter 4

The Many Faces of Challenge: It Comes in All Shapes, Sizes, and Forms

*Every adversity, every failure, every heartache carries
with it a seed of equal or greater benefit.*

—Napoleon Hill

S ome challenges are obvious: losing a job, fighting a
battle with your bodyweight, or perhaps dealing
with a terrible breakup. But other challenges are hidden,
like the limiting beliefs that are part of your subconscious
operating system. These core beliefs were forged through
years of practice and behavior. In either case, challenges
(and the experiences they bring) are yours and yours
alone. No two challenges are the same. Every person experiences adversity and faces challenges in their own
unique way. While this book is meant to be an example of
how to overcome any type of adversity, large or small, I

do not mean to compare my problems to yours. In and of itself, comparison does nothing but compound the pain you are already experiencing.

We learned earlier that one of the key aspects of building resilience is self-care, reaching out, and relying on others to help you overcome your adversity. We have to be able to do this without shame and with a strong conviction that you need help, and your caring friends are the ones to provide it. In all my experience with adversity, I recognize that asking for help was just as important as surrender. In fact, it was in surrendering that I was able to ask for help without shame. Remember that surrendering is not giving up. It is giving in. And there is no shame in giving in, especially when you are doing so to move forward with new purpose and perspective.

There is no shame in getting help. After all, no matter what type of adversity you are experiencing, you must overcome it to build resilience so you can be ready for the next life event. What if I was too ashamed to take that one-hundred-yard walk to my first AA meeting? Where would I be? Would I have the life I have now? Absolutely not. I would still be an alcoholic struggling to survive. Do not let shame keep you from taking action to ask for help.

Shame is an unpleasant, self-conscious emotion associated with a negative evaluation of the self. It is important to acknowledge and process shame so that we can grow and progress as healthy human beings. Nineteenth-century scientist Charles Darwin described shame's effects on your physical form: blushing, downward-cast eyes, slack posture, and lowered head. It is not just something felt, it is also something seen. This is where we need to be mindful of our physiology, and how others might see us. We need to act with conviction to be bold and brave in all we do. Hold your head up high and know that by reaching out for help, you are not giving up. Rather, you are giving in, ready to grow, ready to learn and tap into your superhero mindset so you can overcome.

It has been said that shame, fear, and guilt are the unholy trinity that will continue to drag you down and keep you from moving forward.[9]

The Four Steps to Build Your Resiliency Muscle

According to noted author and phycologist Brené Brown, shame causes people to feel "trapped, powerless, and isolated." Her research explores how people overcome feelings of shame when facing adversity and building resilience. She proposes that shame resilience is essentially made up of four steps:

1. Recognizing the personal vulnerability that led to the feelings of shame
2. Recognizing the external factors that led to the feelings of shame
3. Connecting with others to receive and offer empathy and
4. Discussing and deconstructing the feelings of shame[10]

---

[9] Cliff, "Universal Indicators of Shame—A Blend of Sadness and Embarrassment," August 6th, 2018, https://www.eiagroup.com/universal-indicators-shame-blend-sadness-embarrassment.

[10] Brown, Brené, "Rising Strong: How the Ability to Reset Transforms the Way We Live, Love, Parent, and Lead," April 4, 2017, Random House.

Let us break this down as it relates to how I built resilience and experienced vulnerability in my life. When I think about the four steps of shame, I consider how they presented themselves to me. They forced me to my knees and pushed me to develop—even become—vulnerable, whether I liked it or not.

First, you should accept your negative experience and surrender to it. Only then can you grow and move on. This is all part of being self-aware and knowing that even if you could control what happened, there is no reason to feel shameful or believe that you are less adequate or capable. Everyone is on a level playing field when it comes to this. What separates us is how we deal with it. Maybe you remember that famous quote from *Rocky*: "But it ain't how hard you hit; it's about how hard you can get hit and keep moving forward. How much you can take and keep moving forward. That's how winning is done."

Next, you have to recognize the external factors at play. In this case, we are referring to your limiting beliefs. I call these your "enough statements." If you tell yourself, "I am not good enough," "I am not smart enough," "I am not educated enough," or "I am not worthy enough," then you will start to believe it. These beliefs then become part of your DNA. We all need to break through these limiting beliefs to prove they are not real. Rather, they are just a byproduct of the negative story we tell ourselves.

The next step we can take to build up our resilience to handle adversity is through connecting with others and having a mindset to serve. For me, this means I get out of my self-absorption, help others, and contribute to society. Once you live a life of giving, everything changes. In that moment, you can focus on helping others, rather than fixating on your pain. It should be no mystery that we are all in this together. Through thick and thin, we all share the common pain of challenge. You must get out of the comfort zone of selfishness and think of others first. My belief is that if I show up every day and make the choice to serve and give back to the universe, then the universe will give me exactly what I need. Do not be ashamed of being a loving, giving person. No matter what the relationship, whether work or personal, go into it to give rather than to get. I can tell you from experience that doing this will change every relationship in your life.

Lastly, we all should discuss our feelings as they often relate to shame. You cannot get through challenging life events alone. When I look back over my life, I see my friends and family around me, lifting me up, showing me support. Vulnerability is not a weakness; rather, it is the pathway to courage. Reaching out for help is a sign of strength and self-awareness. On some occasions, it is our feeling of shame that stops us from being vulnerable. But once we shed that shame and open up to those around us and welcome in the challenges, we can begin to grow and move forward.

A few years ago, I wanted to get out of my comfort zone. I decided to take a comedy-writing workshop course to improve my speaking skills. It just so happens that the payoff was a stand-up set at the famous Improv in Atlanta, Georgia. By payoff, I mean horrifying conclusion to months of training. The course was very intense and by far one of the toughest things I have ever done. I spent nine full weeks honing my writing craft and getting ready for my debut on stage. When the big night arrived, I was terrified. There were twelve of us who would perform that night to a packed house. In my set, I talked about AA and my Tourette syndrome, focusing on very personal issues and making light of them. It was downright horrifying. Now, put yourself in the crowd for the night. Would you say I showed weakness or courage? I would argue that each performer showed a tremendous amount of courage by opening our hearts to the audience and being vulnerable. We each shed our shame and faced our fear.

I learned not to shy away from being vulnerable and had a blast while doing so. I also checked one off my bucket list. To this day, people mention that they saw the routine and got a kick out of it. It is out there for all to see, including those I work with in the business world. You would be surprised how many top executives I meet who tell me how much they enjoyed seeing me on stage. They could tell I was having tons of fun. Never underestimate the power of vulnerability and never be ashamed to take the risk—go for it and move forward with new purpose and perspective. After all, you cannot build resilience by standing still.

As a child, I had severe learning disabilities that affected my ability to do well in school. Because of this, I became comfortable with asking for help without shame, realizing I could not do it myself. This is also part of the process of surrender. We should open our hearts and minds to receive the lessons and signs that come our way. I call these God moments, and they allow us to learn, pivot, and take positive from the negative in our life.

But it is not just about God moments happening; we should be awake to life and watching for them. I use the analogy of driving down the highway. Cars are passing you at different speeds, and some are coming the opposite way. Most of the time, you don't even notice. What if we took the time to notice, to be open to the possibilities that may exist out there? We need to open our hearts and catch those God moments that might be passing us by. It doesn't take the catastrophic experience of losing someone you love to wake up and grow. You can pay attention now.

When faced with adversity, many get stuck in shock or anger, blaming others for where they are and how they feel. All that negativity goes away once you surrender. When you take responsibility and become humble, you will find yourself willing to learn, grow, pivot, and take massive action. In my opinion, this choice must be deliberate and conscious. You must want it and work at it. One of the toughest days of my life was the day I got on my knees, surrendered, and asked for help in AA. Ultimately, that action not only changed my life but saved it as well.

My advice: Don't compare or measure yourself against others; measure yourself against you. You are your own competition. *Where* do you want to be? *Who* do you want to be? You need to trust the process and let the results take care of themselves. Bottom line, you need to turn it over, let it go, and trust that you will overcome. In the end, you can only control what is controllable. I learned a long time ago that I cannot control people, places, or things, but I can control how I react to them.

All Adversity Builds Resilience

In my life, I have faced life-altering events, but even the little bumps in the road helped me build up resilience. When I was first starting out in sales, it seemed like the end of the world when I would lose a sale. But once I focused on learning from the experience and becoming more effective, it all changed for me. I built a growth mindset even at a young age. I understood that every moment can be a teaching moment if you cultivate the proper mindset.

It is important to reflect on each setback so you can learn and grow. This gets easier when you accept that where you are is exactly where you need to be. I know the adversity I faced at a young age and throughout my life prepared me for one of the most impactful life events of them all: losing my spouse. I ask you to learn from my experience and take that knowledge with you to your next life event.

For example, when I was in high school, I had the ability to sing and act. I was very active in the theatre and choral group. Every year we would put on a full-scale Broadway musical, complete with an orchestra. I landed a decent part during my sophomore year in the musical *My Fair Lady*, and that kicked off my love for the performing arts. I studied singing outside of school and started performing professionally at weddings and events around Boston. When I wasn't on the basketball court, I was taking voice lessons. When it came time to audition during my junior year for the musical, I went for the lead role of Curly, so famously played by Broadway legend Gordon MacRae, I was so confident that I would land it that I didn't audition for any other role.

Sadly, I did not get the role. Because of my arrogance, I ended up sitting out for the production, watching from the sidelines. I was devastated. I had the bug, and I wanted to be on stage and get that high from the audience. I faced a difficult decision. Would I blame everyone else for what happened and stay in a state of negativity? Or would I move on, take action, and ensure that it didn't happen again? I was young and emotional at the time. So, to be honest, it took me a while to get to the right place. But my mindset changed once I realized I had to take responsibility. I worked even harder on my craft, to be ready for the next year.

Failing to secure the role was not a life-or-death kind of adversity, yet it was life changing for me. It meant something to me as I was going through it because I allowed myself to experience my experience. When something hits you, no matter how small or how large, recognize the pain, deal with it, learn from it, and grow.

Let's take this example and apply the six key aspects of building resilience. In my case, I had to be self-aware enough to realize I wasn't ready to take on a lead role. I had to accept that I was right where I needed to be, working on my craft to get better. Mindfulness allowed me to put things in perspective and come back to the present moment, not dwelling on the past. I put my focus on the goals at hand rather than wallowing in what should have been. I also had to take ownership and not have a victim mentality. I tried to stay in a positive mindset, not blaming others but focusing on what I wanted to accomplish. Positive relationships were also crucial in navigating this setback. When this happened, I surrounded myself with better voice coaches. I turned to my friends and family to keep me positive and grounded; all reminded me that I could do this.

In terms of purpose, I came out of this experience with new purpose, to get better and land the lead role the next year. And finally, perhaps the most important step in my progression was finding the courage to surrender. This was my ability to give in, accept I was not ready, and work on becoming ready. I had to surrender to the fact that I was right where I needed to be. As it turns out, during my senior year I got the lead role in *Carousel* of Billy Bigelow that was originally performed on Broadway, again, by Gordon MacRae. I had a great experience, and the show got a standing ovation. We had an amazing cast, and some of my best memories are of that time.

The Smallness of Adversity

On most occasions, we experience small adversity, not the large type. It is not in the big life events we build resilience, although they certainly put us on a fateful crash course with it. Rather, we build resilience daily by surviving the small things. The key here is to understand the importance of facing and learning from all your moments. You don't have to experience a God moment to learn resilience. In fact, it is the non-God moments that prepare you for the big swings and the greatest surrender.

Through practicing mindfulness, I have learned to be present in the moment and grateful for all life has given me. I have learned to keep my eyes open, ready to grow from each and every experience. Every day, we have a choice to live in a beautiful state or not. We have a choice to be in the moment and present or distracted and stuck. Mindfulness is a game-changer, for sure. AA taught me to not obsess over what could or might happen but to live my best life in the moment.

When I first went into AA and realized I could never have another drink, I was depressed that I would not be able to toast my daughter at her wedding. She was nine at the time. Of course, when she did eventually get married, I was able to toast her and my new son-in-law; I just did it with sparkling apple juice. At the wedding, I laughed to myself, remembering how concerned I was about making it through my daughter's big day without alcohol. When her wedding finally arrived, my beverage at the toast was insignificant. It is all about perspective. Every experience in your life has impact, and you can choose if it is positive or negative.

So, open your heart to the moments in which you can

learn. They are coming at us quickly, and if you aren't careful, you will miss them. To build resilience and to thrive again, you need to capture these moments, acknowledge them, and attach them to your new unlimited beliefs.

Surrender Is the Path Out

With surrender, you take responsibility; you become humble and willing to learn, to grow, to pivot and take massive action. This is a deliberate and conscious action. You must want it and work at it. Remember, surrender isn't easy. It is painful and extremely scary to give in something you have known for so long. When I recognized I had no control over my drinking, I saw I must surrender it. That decision changed my life and is an example of the type of unparalleled power surrender can offer you. Even when we have small setbacks, it is important to reflect and grow from them.

Surrender is truly the only way forward. I have a choice to live each day in a positive state or a negative state, a choice to focus on what I have or what I don't have. In AA, I learned to check my expectations and be grateful. In other words, I can fight my circumstance, or I can surrender to it and give in each day to the notion that "it is what it is." I cannot control people, places, and things. By surrendering, I can start each day in gratitude. I can move on from the noise of the media and thrive. I know this will pass and fighting it will not make it go away more quickly. I can only control what I can control. I work to stay healthy, practicing the principles scientists have suggested, and I live in the moment, letting the noise pass me by. Remember, surrender is not giving up; it is giving in. I am thriving in 2020 and finding a way to live in the positive. When I have my moments of despair, I use what I have learned to snap out of it. I reach out to others, and I serve.

Though I didn't need one more reason to write this book, the worldwide pandemic was a not-so-subtle reminder that we have little control over our life experiences. Sure, we can choose how we respond and act when troubles present themselves. But unless we surrender to the adversity we face, we stand no chance to course correct and handle the challenges. Adversity comes in many different shapes and sizes, but each trial presents the opportunity to learn, grow, and come out better than when we started. But our response determines if we will take the opportunity presented. So welcome adversity as a meaningful and natural part of your life.

chapter 5

Hidden in Darkness: Understanding Adversity's Impact on Your Life

Challenges are what make life interesting,
overcoming them is what makes life meaningful.

—Joshua J. Marine

T hrough all my experiences, I have learned that life is happening to strengthen me, not to break me. Once you come to that same valuable realization, you will notice that everything changes. You will look at life in a whole new way; you will see more purpose and meaning. In this new-found narrative, your first step will be to identify the adversity in your life. That is also the first step in surrendering to the journey you will ultimately experience. You cannot have surrender without awareness, which enables you to recognize the presence and root of your adversity. In this chapter, we will focus on building our awareness of adversity and seek to better understand how adversity impacts our life.

Let's begin with a closer look at how adversity will likely show up in your life. It predictably arrives in these forms:

1. Hidden stress in life, work, and family
2. Self-induced pressure
3. Lack of action
4. Addiction to the negative
5. Uncontrollable elements in the environment

At first glance, these sources of adversity seem like common sense. But when you are walking through a rough patch, it may not be so obvious. As the old saying goes, "You can't see the forest for the trees." For example, the basic stress of life, work, and family can build up over time. If not addressed, you may find yourself boiling over. Dealing with this kind of adversity is not something people often talk about. Adversity always seems to be about the massive life events, like losing a spouse or a child, a failed marriage, or a major health scare. But we often overlook the small stressors that add up to pain. The question now should be, how do we handle the everyday adversity right in front of us? You should put your life, work, family stress into perspective. Although some people do have highly stressful jobs, most of us are not solving world hunger or performing brain surgery. The task at hand will be there tomorrow, and if it's not done, no one will die.

Just the other day, my stepdaughter had on a T-shirt that said (in capital letters), "BUT DID YOU DIE?" We tend to

SURRENDER TO YOUR ADVERSITY

create our own drama, our own narrative of stress. I say this because I believe we have a choice when it comes to the kind of stress we introduce into our lives. It may seem very strange to you, but losing my wife, Bonnie, changed me overnight, offering up an unexpected, and certainly unwelcomed, new perspective on life. Today, I continue to strive to make living in a beautiful state non-negotiable.

I have come to realize that I need to reprioritize what was truly important. But you can use big and small events to change your perspective. You will be surprised how the universe will reward you for this approach. Most of the time when I mentor people, we talk about the stress they put on themselves. Although it is good to be driven, it is also good to drive safely. The famous quote, "Go slow to go fast," says it all. Slow down and you can go faster, farther, and with greater purpose.

So, how do we use adversity to build resilience for when we really need it? Think about it like this. No one can be fully prepared for losing a loved one, navigating a serious health scare, or getting fired from your job. In each of those scenarios, you will inevitably face a series of ups and downs. No matter how resilient you are, the pain will certainly cut deep, possibly plunging you into depression. It takes time to heal. These are not the moments that fill our resilience tanks. But the smaller moments, like overcoming a self-limiting belief, navigating a new opportunity, dealing with everyday frustrations or with not getting a raise or a promotion, are the occasions to bank a full tank of resilience.

"Stress isn't always harmful,"[11] says Kelly McGonigal, a business school lecturer at Stanford University and

---

[11] http://kellymcgonigal.com.

program developer for the Stanford Center for Compassion and Altruism Research and Education. "Once you appreciate that going through stress makes you better at it, it can be easier to face each new challenge." This is a mindset you need to work on. It is yours for the taking, but you absolutely must take it.

Next time you experience stress, step into it. Acknowledge it and appreciate it as something that will make you stronger. Our brain only knows fight or flight; there has been no upgrade since the caveman. You need to reprogram your brain to accept and appreciate stress as a learning experience. By doing this, you can thank your brain for making you pay attention. Only then can you look at your options and start to formulate an action plan. The fact is, there is always a path forward. It may seem silly at first, but it is important to acknowledge this out loud and so program the belief into your subconscious. Doing this will help you deal with stress. And as McGonigal points out, there is such a thing as "good stress." It's the kind of stress that keeps us focused and on point and makes us take action.

In Netflix series, *The Playbook*, showcasing the world's best professional coaches and their rules for life, Doc Rivers, a Hall of Famer NBA basketball coach, shares one of his five rules to success. He states, "Pressure is a privilege." Those are words to live by. Pressure makes us stronger, and in the long run, it builds up our resilience for the next challenge. I stress this with those I mentor, my employees, and my children. Learn to use pressure as a positive growth experience, learning from each scenario and using it to fill up your resilience tank.

It all comes down to living in the present moment, which gives us great opportunity to resolve any immediate pain.

My good friend Russ Rausch, founder of Vision Pursue LLC, talks about living your life through the eyes of a dog. A dog sees only the present moment and takes in all the good. If you take your dog on a walk, he will see the sun, the trees, and the squirrels. He will be in the moment. We are on the same walk with the same view, but we are on the phone or thinking of work or worrying about the weather tomorrow. We miss the moment by worrying about the future. Russ and his team have helped executives, pro athletes, and others reprogram their brain with Vision Pursue.

Russ also speaks of controlling the controllable. In AA we focus on what we control and let the rest go. We do this twenty-four hours at a time—or one day at a time, as the saying goes. Doing this one thing, learning to stay in the moment, can help reduce the stress we put on ourselves. So, the next time you are on a walk, make it a point to be in the moment. Check out Vision Pursue at www.visionpursue.com and get started on your new mindset.

Enjoy the present and give yourself permission to experience the simple task of just taking a walk. If you really want to step it up, you can use apps to do a mindful meditation while you walk. Make sure to put your phone on do not disturb before you try it, though; you don't want to ruin the experience with a phone call or text that can absolutely wait. I make it a point to "check out" a few times a day. Sometimes it's only for fifteen minutes, but my phone is off, and I am unplugged. I find it a much-needed reset that I don't do often enough. When we practice this and are truly present with ourselves, our heart can open and we can accept those gifts that come to us, maybe a God moment.

At about a year and half sober, I was traveling back to

New York after working on a deal that I really had to close. We were in the middle of a heated negotiation with this rather large financial institution. Unfortunately, we weren't getting anywhere. It was the end of the year, and time was running out for me. I needed to come up with a solution. I remember pacing outside on the streets of Manhattan and reciting the serenity prayer repeatedly. The prayer saved me before, and I figured it would do so again. Shortly after, the lead council called me and offered to step in to help me get the deal over the line. Her name was Judith. For some reason we made an instant human connection and we spoke for some time about the issues I was facing. She knew I was stressed, so I shared a bit of my story with her and let her know that we needed to get this deal closed before Christmas. She told me to take a deep breath, relax, and trust her. Judith and I worked nonstop to get the final deal in place. We completed it in the nick of time.

But that is not where the story ends. Now, here is the God moment. I reached back out to Judith after the holidays. She was nowhere to be found. I searched for her and had other employees at the bank try to locate her. After all my best efforts, I never was able to get back in touch. I am not sure what exactly happened to me that last week of the year, but in that moment, I decided to live in faith not fear. I looked for God moments, grabbed them, and learned from them. I am forever grateful to receive these gifts.

It is not just the adversity that rocks your world or gives you no alternative but to act. Little things can add up and eventually take you to a place where you cannot see the light at the end of the tunnel. It can be a slow descent, like death by a million papercuts. The key is to develop the ability to recognize, accept, surrender, and act quickly.

A lack of action will keep you from the ability to

surrender. Pain is in our lives not to make us suffer. It is there to push us to act. But you should do the work and move forward. You should give in and start to pivot with new purpose. Being an addict, I know too well that it comes down to how much pain you will endure before you take action to get better and end your suffering. You can heal once you make that decision. I have seen many people sit in their pain and not act. They can't see the way through. The sad truth is it doesn't take a massive pivot. You can see results and build momentum with the little things you do to move forward. When I was first getting sober, I focused on staying sober for one day at a time, just twenty-four-hour increments on my way to a lifetime of sobriety. It was the only way I knew to do it. How do you eat an eight-thousand-pound elephant? One bite at a time.

I built momentum after I put together twenty-four-hour chunks. As I am writing these words, I have over twenty-seven years of sobriety, and it all started with that small step to just stay sobor for one day. But it's not just about being sober. Frankly, you can apply this practice to any meaningful marathon goal. Consider the decision to lose weight. Try to set the goal and celebrate the wins along the way. Maybe you want to lose twenty-five pounds. You can't do that in one week, but you can set a goal of something more manageable. You can aim to lose a pound a week and then celebrate that win. It will add up, and you will reach your goal. Momentum is the key to acting. Reaching long-term goals is just a function of reaching a bunch of short-term goals. As you stack them, they add up.

When I was twenty-three years old, I had just graduated from college and was looking for a job. Bonnie and I were married and about to celebrate our one-year anniversary.

I sent my résumé out to dozens of companies but didn't get even one reply. I was in our one-room apartment in the suburbs of Boston, sitting in my comfort zone of negativity, blaming everyone else for my lack of success. Bonnie looked at me and said, "What are *you* doing to get a job? Sitting here is not going to make it happen, so get out there and sell yourself." She was right, so I decided to hit the pavement and personally deliver my résumé to a bunch of prospective employers. It wasn't long before I met and befriended a headhunter who saw potential in me and helped me land my first job out of college, which started my career in business.

Let's talk about being addicted to the negative. Have you made the negative, or depression, your comfort zone? It takes effort to stay in the negative and take no action. It is hard work to blame the world for your problems; it is draining. You may be surprised, but I believe it takes more energy to be in a negative state than in a state of positivity. Even worse, negativity can become addictive. Just as you can be addicted to the high you get from going to the gym, running, and eating healthy, you can also become addicted to the lows. You choose the state you are in. You choose your path forward—just you and no one else. I speak from experience as someone once fully addicted to my own depression. It became my comfort zone, and at my lowest point, it felt so familiar that it was hard to see a way out.

Consider this: We are all magnets, attracting what we put out into the world. If we are projecting negative thoughts and feelings, we will attract those types of people, and we will continue to live in a negative space. We will live in fear and not faith. If you are one of these people, I get it. I was you. So, I completely understand. I lived in the negative and found myself addicted to being sad. I could be found marinating in my fear and my negative talk.

How crazy is that? But I had trained my brain to go negative. This was an acceptable state to me. I sat on the pity potty, expecting the world to solve my problems. I was convinced that life was happening to me and not for me. Know this: you are not alone. Like me, you can change your perspective. Once you understand that you are surrounded by opportunities, you can open your heart and start to recognize them. Do that, and the world is at your fingertips.

I also got in this negative space when, at one point in my life, we lost our house, went bankrupt, and were out of options. It just seemed easier to give up. But—are you ready for this?—it got easier when I surrendered and figured out a way to move forward. I wrote down a plan to be deliberate in my intentions. I started small and gathered the momentum I talk about so much.

You see, it only takes a minor shift in your state to get massive results. You just need to start. You may have heard the saying, "As long as you are moving forward, it is always better than standing still." I truly believe that sentiment. Once I made the choice to move forward, all that was left to do was the action.

It has been almost one year since we arrived in London, and we have been in and out of lockdown for most of it. My London office has been closed for all but my first three weeks after arrival. Throughout my time here, I have had to adapt and find new ways to make a connection. In fact, I have yet to meet many team members here, face-to-face. This has created issues, as it is ideal to build a strong culture of trust and collaboration while delivering revenue to the company. But I was absolutely prepared for this moment. All the adversity in my life so far has gotten me ready for this moment and, frankly, for any other moment I might face.

Now more than ever, I am confident that I am equipped with a full tank of resilience and have the tools to get through anything. I have a mindset that will allow me to overcome, and a support system to help me thrive. All I need to do is make up my mind to live in a beautiful state, to serve others, and be grateful for the little things, not just the big ones. The same can be, and should be, true for you. Separate that which you can control from that which you cannot control. The lessons you learn from past adversity don't seem that important until you string them together to face the next challenge. For example, in AA I learned to focus on the moment, the day, the next twenty-four hours. By doing this, I was beginning to practice a state of mindfulness, staying in the moment, controlling only what I could, and letting the rest go.

Now, I could watch the news every single day, spend time on social media, and worry about what might happen. Or I can take an entirely different route by living my best life now, present in the moment. I can obsess about the future and stay in the negative, or I can put out positive vibes and get out of myself, help others, and let the rest fall into place. You see, I was ready for COVID-19, and I am dealing with it the only way I know how. I have given in to it, and am living in faith, not fear. I know that I will be just fine. This too shall pass, and I will come out the other end stronger, better, and in a place of strength. The rise is always sweeter than the fall.

Why do I know all of this? Because I made the decision to move, adapt, and pivot. I'll come out of this adversity with new purpose and perspective. I can tell you one thing for sure; I am now so grateful to have any human connection, and I look forward to returning to some sort of normal again. Before, social connection was a way of life, something I took for granted. Now, it is a conscious and concerted effort to do so safely.

If we so determine, we can all come out of each adversarial experience with new purpose and perspective. The ones who will struggle are those who decide to remain in the negative space, blaming others and fighting an enemy they can't even see. They waste all their energy on negativity, choosing not to serve, refusing to live in gratitude, and of course, obsessing on the negative. I feel for them; I really do. We all have an important choice to make, and it is up to each of us to make the right one. To serve your greatest purpose, do not let any experience of adversity go by without learning something you can bring forward.

We do this through recognizing our adversity, understanding it, and coming to terms with it. First Lady Michelle Obama said, "You should never view your challenges as a disadvantage. Instead, it's important for you to understand that your experience facing and overcoming adversity is actually one of your biggest advantages."[12] I could not agree more. Let adversity live in your life, but don't allow it to control you. Choose to face it with courage, for when you decide to live in your adversity, you become more likely to overcome it.

---

[12] McClain, Oscar, "Turning Adversities into Inspiration," November 8, 2019, https://www.forbes.com/sites/civicnation/2019/11/08/turning-adversities-into-inspiration/?sh=29d310aa6513.

chapter 6

Into the Light: Bringing Adversity to a Place of Clarity

*Hardships often prepare ordinary people for an
extraordinary destiny.*

—C. S. Lewis

From darkness to light: this is where the shift occurs. In this chapter, we bridge the gap between the two; we will shed the challenge of adversity and move into a place of clarity. To this point in the book, we have discussed that which causes our pain, looking back to its origins. But, recognizing you have pain (or problems that generate pain) is often the first step in your evolution and development. As we manifest that portion of our journey, we can turn adversity into a character quality, something we can use as a tool and resource in our battle against limiting beliefs and experiences. My dad always told me, "Adversity builds character." I would always come back with, "I think I have enough character now, Dad."

It is not always easy to surrender to the pain of an unknown and seemingly never-ending situation. However, pain remains as the number one path to growth—or at least the fastest route. You can fight and fight and fight the pain, but you will never get to the place you want to be if you stay stuck in the struggle. We all want to live in the light, and this chapter will help you to do that by outlining the powerful steps you can take to cross the bridge from darkness to a life filled with light.

Let Resilience Be Your Flashlight

Resilient people generally recognize the difference between right and wrong as they typically carry a strong moral compass. They believe in something greater than themselves, a higher power. This is not a religious statement but a spiritual one. To surrender, you need to believe in a higher power. That is really the whole point. Every time adversity brought me to my knees, I was humbled by a power greater than myself. It was that power that gave me the strength to stand again on my own.

You have read about my bouts of adversity. Now, I want to share the tricks I learned to ultimately surrender. Doing so opened my heart and mind so I could grow, thrive again, and live a life I never could have imagined. This is probably a good time to let you know that my love story did not end the day my beloved Bonnie passed in that hospital room.

I had so much support from my friends after Bonnie's passing. They would take turns keeping me busy, making sure I was not sitting at home alone in that big house. My friends kept me busy with all sorts of activities, like walks, runs, yoga, lunches, dinners, and nights out; you name it, and they thought of it. Afterall, they were trying to show their support and love during this difficult time. One of our friends, Missy, kept me busy, going to the gym or doing yoga classes. She encouraged me to eat healthy and take care of myself when I just wanted to give up. Missy had been Bonnie's good friend and was recently divorced herself, so she had time to watch out for me. We were always close, a relationship built on friendship. Bonnie would joke that if anything ever happened to her, Missy would be her choice for me to find love again.

Bonnie and I met Missy when our kids were carpooling to a local private school. We would take turns driving all five kids between us. Missy and her husband would come to our parties at the pool, and Bonnie and Missy had a connection. They both had raised children with complications at a young age. Missy's son, Matt, had brain cancer as a baby and beat it, and, of course, Bonnie had Eric. They bonded with the common goal to be an advocate for their children.

The first year after Bonnie's passing was a total blur. Time moved yet seemed to stand still. It was a strange experience. I was beginning to thrive in business and get back on track, but I was still trying to find my new normal, whatever that meant. Missy was one of many friends who kept me on track and moving forward, even if I was only taking baby steps. I didn't date at all during the first year and never really thought about it. I spent time with women, but they were friends. I would go to concerts or out dancing or to dinner, and over time I came out of my shell a bit and had fun again.

On the one-year anniversary of Bonnie's passing, we planned to spread her ashes at Chappaquiddick on

Martha's Vineyard. Bonnie had spent most of her summers there. It was her happy place, becoming ours after we got married. To me it is one of the most beautiful places on earth. I made the journey from Atlanta with my kids, and we rented a boat to take about thirty of us around the tip of the island to where she wanted to rest. It was a magical day without a cloud in the sky. We spent time on the beach reflecting on her life, telling stories, laughing, crying, and remembering the beautiful soul she was to all of us.

It was strange to be on the Vineyard without Bonnie for the first time in my life. I remember taking the ferry from Cape Cod to the island and at one point just breaking down. My kids surrounded me and comforted me as I wept on the top deck of the ferry. It was just too overwhelming for me to take anymore. I was grateful to have my kids and close friends and family with me that day to help me get through it. My kids were so strong, and we spent the week together going to the beach and to our favorite spots on the cape and island.

I returned to Atlanta in August to an empty house. But this time it was different. I felt like I finally had some closure. Spreading her ashes was liberating. I knew she was at peace where she always wanted to rest. I felt I had done all I could for me, the kids, and our friends. It was when I returned from the Cape that I felt different, like I could move forward with Bonnie beside me. A few weeks later, I called the kids together and asked if it was okay with them to think of dating. They were all behind me getting back to life and finding someone to spend time with.

I am sure Bonnie was smiling above when I came up with the idea to ask Missy out on a date, which was not an easy thing to do. I hadn't asked a woman out since I was nineteen years old. How was this going to work anyway? I went to the best source I knew for advice: my two boys. They were so excited that Missy was my love interest. In fact, their first reaction was, "We love Missy; you have to ask her out, Dad." I then turned to my daughter. She had the same reaction. Lastly, I called Bonnie's mom—who, by any account, was my mom as well. Nat and I are extremely close and talk about everything. I told her my plan. She was elated. I remember her saying to me, "Don't you dare spend any more time alone; you need to be with someone." She also knew Missy and loved her as well.

After mulling it over, I got the nerve to ask Missy on a date. She said yes, and we began to date. There is a lesson here for anyone trying to get back to normal after a loss of great significance. Though you may get mixed reactions from family and friends, you must stay true to your feelings. You need to move on with the person you choose. Missy and I dated for a couple of years. In 2016, three years after Bonnie passed, we got married. We had our closest friends and family there, and it was a magical day. It was hard to believe that I would be so lucky to find love again in my life, but I did. Bonnie was there that day, making sure the weather was perfect and that everything went off without a hitch.

When we got our photos back from that day, we noticed one shot, in particular. It was of us taking our vows. When we looked closer, we noticed a halo enveloping both Missy and me. Yes, she was there, and she is still with us, watching over us and our crazy blended family. The point in sharing this story of resilience with you is that I want to remind you to open your heart, no matter how hurt you might be. Living with a closed heart is no way to go through life. I don't want to imagine my life without Missy and without the chance to find love again. A true example of how to make living in a beautiful state non-negotiable.

Values Create Clarity

I have found that morals often help create clarity around challenges and adversity. Today, my values are all about making a human connection with others, living a life of giving, always having a growth mindset, and living in a state of gratitude every day. These values guide my decisions, my attitude, the actions I take, and the people I surround myself with. They dictate my priorities and reinforce my purpose. It takes work, but we can get to this place if we take action. This does not happen overnight, and it comes with some soul searching for sure, but I speak from experience that it is worth it. When I took the time to work on myself and really understand what was important to me, the world changed.

A door opened with each passing challenge. With each experience came a new vision, new paths, and a new purpose. When I walked into the rooms of AA for the first time, I understood just what this all means. And when I lost Bonnie and had to face one of the biggest tests of all, I understood what it meant to drop to my knees and surrender, to give in and enable myself to reset, change direction, and move forward. After all, that is what we have been talking about here: the ability to act when you face adversity, to surrender and cash in on the resilience you have been building up by learning from the events in life, small and large.

The sooner you come to terms with the fact that life is happening to make you stronger, the better life will be. Don't be the victim, don't blame others for the decisions you made, and don't expect anyone else to put you on the right path. Support from others is a key aspect of facing adversity, but you are the one who needs to take the action here. You should want it, and you have to live it. So many people say they want to change, take action, face their fears, and overcome adversity, but few will put the work in to succeed.

Living a Life in the Light

Let's talk about living in the light, about living the life you deserve and, honestly, have earned. You make decisions every day: What state do you want to live in? What attitude are you going to project? And, if you get in the negative, how long are you going to allow yourself to stay in that state? Have you heard of the ninety-second rule? I can be pissed, sad, negative, upset, and frustrated but for only ninety seconds. Then I snap my fingers and am back to living in a beautiful state. Now, this takes a lot of practice, but I have that mindset and continue to work on it. This is a lifelong journey, so don't think you are going to conquer this overnight. Like my sobriety, I take these steps one day at a time. I practice progress rather than perfection.

When does this shift happen? When do you finally figure out how to live in the right place? The answer is simple: it is when you do the work. It does not come to you. In my case, I have done and continue to do a lot of personal development. I live in a growth mindset, always learning, always moving out of my comfort zone. I mean, I have never written a book before and look at me now. I am getting my story out there so you can learn from my experience. As I said before, everyone has a story to write, but you should try to get out of your comfort zone to do it.

Let me share a few steps I take every day to live in a beautiful state. My experience tells me that if you focus your energy on these three basic actions, you will always overcome and thrive again, even after major adversity.

Open your heart and accept grace. Choose to live a life of faith not fear. Carl Jung, Swiss psychiatrist, once advised us to look inside ourselves for the answers: "Your vision will become clear only when you look into your heart . . . Who looks outside, dreams. Who looks inside, awakens." This is the way to move forward after surrender. Be vulnerable and be authentic. You may have heard this saying before, but I try and surround myself with three kinds of people:

1. The inspired
2. The excited
3. The grateful

In my most tragic life events, it always came down to this. I had to look inside myself and decide what actions I was going to take, what attitude I was going to have, and, most important, I had to clarify my vision moving forward. Where do I want to be and what life do I want for myself? In doing this, I had to search my soul and work on myself. This can be achieved through personal development, such as reading self-help books and applying their content or attending therapy sessions with a professional who can help you understand these concepts and how to apply them to your life. It also helps to surround yourself with positive influences. You will always take on the attitude of those around you, so choose your circle wisely.

As I write this book, many of us are navigating the challenging times 2020 has brought. Focus and positive attitude is now more important than ever. I know for a fact I need to be surrounded by the positive. I need to be a magnet for the positive and live a life of gratitude every day. You may need to limit your time on social media and be more present for your loved ones. Or you may begin a daily meditation practice to ground yourself prior to starting the day. Or maybe you will take a run in the morning, work out, or do yoga. Whatever works, keep doing it.

Create your own destiny. Tony Robbins reminds us that, "It is in your moments of decision that your destiny is shaped. Make the decision to shape your own destiny, to discover your purpose in life and learn what truly motivates you. Realign your values and start living the life you desire and deserve." This takes work and soul searching. You have to do this with full conviction. Know that the journey will be difficult but worth it.

I have had the opportunity twice in my life to walk over fire. For those who have done this, you know that the only way to survive is to walk with conviction and have no fear. You need to put yourself in a peak state that allows you to walk some fifteen feet over sixteen-hundred-degree hot coals and not get burned. As you take this journey (or any journey for that matter), your destiny may eventually change and pivot. That is not important. The key is to keep moving forward, even if with small steps. Moving forward is always better than standing still. By opening your heart to receive grace, giving yourself permission to dream, and by taking action, you can and will create your destiny for an amazing future and life.

Give yourself permission. I will close this chapter with the most important lesson, in my opinion: give yourself permission. As best-selling author and researcher Brené Brown says, "Nothing has transformed my life more than realizing that it's a waste of time to evaluate my worthiness by weighing the reaction of the people in the stands." You cannot be influenced by other people's negative attitude. Give yourself permission to live and thrive again, making no excuses. I will say that after Bonnie passed there were some friends and family who didn't always agree with my decisions. But in the long run, I did what was best for me and my family.

I can remember a few who were vocal when I started dating Missy after a year of being alone. We have seen a similar scenario play out in the media with the story of actor Patton Oswalt who got remarried fifteen months after his first wife has passed. Patton was criticized in the media for moving on too quickly. I understand firsthand what he went through. First, it is no one's business when and how we move forward after loss. The lesson I learned was not to listen to the people in the stands. Instead of listening to them, listen to your heart. Give yourself permission to move on *with* your loved one—not from.

I still feel Bonnie on my shoulder every day, even after eight years. You never move on from that person you lose. They are always part of your heart, and you take them with you as you find your new purpose and start to thrive again. And remember, it takes a special person to come into your life after a loss like that. They should be very comfortable with the fact that there are three people in the relationship because the truth is, you never forget. Your loved one made a stamp on your heart that will be there for eternity.

The same goes with any adversity, not just loss. When I got sober, I gave myself permission to live an awesome life and to thrive without alcohol. I also gave myself permission to distance myself from those who could take me back there. I had to change my hangouts, some of my friends, and, in the end, I had to move from my hometown and start over. I gave myself permission so I could thrive again. I talked about self-care in chapter one as a key element of building resilience. Making changes that were good for my soul is a perfect example of how I cared for myself to get back on track.

My friend Sonia Singh was a shy, scrappy kid. Always the smallest in her class, she was often made fun of for looking different. Racism was alive and well as she grew up in Chicago during the early '80s. Sonia didn't own any name brand clothes, and toys were a scarce luxury her parents could not afford. They were Punjabi immigrants from India, trying their best with what they had. With English as her second language, Sonia also struggled in school. Many of her teachers gave up on her or, worse, forgot she was even there. But that little girl in pigtails started developing grit. She didn't realize it at the time, but she had a superhero inside just waiting to come out.

As she says today, "It's not about lack of resources. It's lack of resourcefulness!" She bartered with other kids, found toys in dumpsters, made allies who were bigger and stronger than her, and stood up for smaller kids who were being picked on. Her mom sewed outfits by hand that looked like brand names. She read the dictionary and other books to increase her vocabulary. She developed negotiation, communication, and entrepreneurial skills. However, Sonia's innate ambition was often stifled by well-meaning adults in her life trying to protect her.

She was told never to ask for more than you get, to be obedient, and stay quiet. This was a cultural cycle of limiting beliefs that was passed down from generation to generation. In her early years, Sonia was invisible. She was taught to believe that success for someone like her—a shy, brown-skinned, immigrant girl—was limited. So, she adopted these beliefs as her own: Go to college, but do not expect to be a top student. Get a good job, but do not expect to be the CEO. Make money, but do not expect to be rich.

But that all changed when Sonia was twenty-four and her older sister went missing for several months. Her sister had special needs, and it devastated Sonia to think of what might happen to her. Her nightmare came true when she found out that her sister had been killed. That was the moment that Sonia called on her superhero mindset and told herself that she was going to change her life and her beliefs. She would use the grit she developed at a young age to take action. She realized that she needed to live life to the fullest because it could end at any point without any warning.

The next few years were dark as she grieved her loss and suffered the depression, pain, and PTSD that came along with it. Through it all, she was determined to keep going. Sonia left home, finished school, and became very successful in corporate life. She became a role model. She channeled her anger about what happened to her sister into a positive mindset and focused on self-care. In January 2004, she wrote in her journal that she would start a new career as a consultant, even though she had no experience or connections. She set a goal to move to either San Francisco, Houston, or Los Angeles by July that year.

On July 1, 2004, Sonia moved to Houston to start her new job as a consultant at a Fortune 200 company. Her ability to manifest, visualize, and create her own destiny was realized. She continued to have a very successful career, got married, and is now raising a family. In 2020, she retired from corporate life to start her next chapter. Sonia is now the founder and CEO of a leadership training, coaching, and consulting company. Just one week after launching her company, her client base built quickly and today enjoys a successful business doing the work she absolutely loves.

Sonia is an adjunct professor at the University of San Francisco, teaches at the University of California, Davis, and is an internationally certified leadership coach who helps dozens of executives every week to tap into their greatness and develop resilience, emotional intelligence, and confidence so they can serve the world with their gifts. She uses the skills she developed in her life to give back and serve others. She sees the suffering, resistance, and conflict in business today and is dedicated to bringing human connection back to the way we interact with each other. One of my favorite quotes from Sonia is, "Grit is a game of resourcefulness. Do what you can with what you have until you get what you want."

We all want to walk in the light. I can tell you from firsthand experience that darkness is not fun. It can be downright miserable. But the way we know the light is to first experience darkness. Light and darkness, like yin and yang, exist in perfect balance, one requiring the other. Think about what it feels like to go from darkness to light. The bright, radiant light pierces through your eyes, causing a reaction that often creates immediate clarity. You can see. You can feel. It all comes into focus. Adversity is the same way. It offers us up a choice: put on the blinders or focus your time and energy on clarity. In the end, like anything in life, the choice is up to you.

chapter 7

Your Journey Is Your Own: The Path to Overcoming Limiting Beliefs

*If you accept a limiting belief, then it will
become a truth for you.*

—Louise Hay

We all have limiting beliefs, thoughts, and ideas that serve no valuable purpose but are leeches that suck away our good intentions and desire to accomplish great things. Whether we like it or not, a negative, limiting voice is often present in our mind. However, if we are going to accomplish anything of great meaning, we must set aside these beliefs and replace them with the strong voice of conviction.

The story you tell yourself is one that has been developing for years, even before your memory. Beliefs form in response to our environment, family life, and the adversity we face. They can become so powerful that they take over your inner voice and make you accept their messages without question. From a young age, I had beliefs telling me that I was stupid, that I would never go to college. In sports, they told me I wasn't good enough, wasn't fast enough, and wasn't a natural athlete. Maybe you have similar limiting beliefs blocking your potential to thrive. As we experience adversity, these beliefs get louder and seem to make sense.

What if I listened to those beliefs, to the negative messages in my mind? Where would I be today? Would I have graduated college and gone on to have the success I now enjoy? Would I have had the confidence to try new things and get out of my comfort zone? If I listened to those voices that told me I was a slow learner and had severe learning disabilities in reading and math, would I be writing this book? I think you know the answer.

The Fault in Our Limiting Beliefs

The truth is, we have all the power and all the tools we need. We just need to enter our mental gym and build up our resilience muscle. Once we do that, there is nothing we cannot accomplish. Maybe you can relate to this. Maybe, like the rest of us, you often find yourself having trouble navigating the tough times. And I would guess that at some point in your life someone told you that you would never be able to (fill in the blank). We have all been there. It is painful to hear that you are not good enough, maybe even from someone you trust. Your decision in that moment will make all the difference in the path your life takes. Here is the good news: you can make a change at any time if you do the work and take massive action toward your new purpose and new perspective. Pain and adversity exist in our life to move us into action and find a new perspective; it's not to make us suffer. We need to run toward the pain, face it, and surrender to it. Then I can move past it by taking massive action.

To overcome limiting beliefs, we must first know what those are for us. This requires self-awareness. We talked about this earlier. Growing in self-awareness means you become aware of the gifts God has given you. It also means becoming aware of where you are letting negative beliefs hold you back. So first, identify your strengths. Then ask, what can I do to stack the deck in my favor? Like me, maybe you have a difficult time retaining what you read or learn. I have conquered that by always carrying a note-book with me and taking good notes that I can refer to later. In fact, I have figured out that I learn better when I write notes, so I sometimes will re-write the notes again a few times to ensure that I retain important facts or figures I need to know in my job. This is part of my self-awareness. I know my strengths and have learned to navigate my weaknesses.

Limiting beliefs aren't necessarily true weaknesses; they are the negative stories we are believing about ourselves, but they may not be true. Thus, limiting beliefs can have a catastrophic impact on how much we achieve. Some say these beliefs protect us from getting hurt by risking too much. After all, they do keep us in our comfort zone. If we don't take action because we believe "I'm too old to start a new career" or "All my relationships fail," then it may seem we protect ourselves from harm in the short term. But these negative scripts can hold us back from reaching our destiny, our true purpose. Our inner voice is strong.

Think of it this way: if you grow up in a house where you are told you are worthless, then it doesn't take long before you believe it. Can you imagine the impact of that statement when you are telling yourself that story? Change your inner voice, change your life. Most limiting beliefs are not accurate, not by the slightest. Only you can know the truth—and that comes through self-awareness. Only you can break down the barrier of those beliefs and find your voice of conviction to overcome those beliefs.

Simone Prinsloo is a true superhero and cancer survivor. As a single mom, the past fourteen years of her life were a constant battle. She feels like she has been in a constant war zone, fighting battles and facing adversity at every turn.

She has made some decisions in the past that she regrets and cannot change. She was happily married and blessed with two beautiful children. Simone has always been an entrepreneur at heart and started her own business, which was successful for fourteen years. She got divorced after seventeen years of marriage, then went into a ten-year relationship of abuse, although her partner never saw it that way. To him, abuse could only be physical, but Simone suffered his emotional abuse. But any abuse is abuse, period.

The first year of the relationship was okay, but then the pain started. Her partner at the time was taking drugs and drinking behind her back; she had no idea how bad it was. Then the lies and cheating started, working late, and addiction to internet porn sites. Her life became a mess to say the least.

Four years ago, Simone was diagnosed with cancer and lost all her hair and her identity. She had major surgery and underwent serious chemo treatments. During this time, she had to shut down her business, which she was so passionate about. That meant limited income coming in, so she lost her home. You can only image the emotional trauma she and her children went through during that time. Simone has always been a very positive person and a fighter. She is a real-life superhero. The only way she survived was by turning to God and living a life of faith, not fear. Simone believes that's what got her through her adversity.

Her old limiting beliefs centered around hurt, pain, bitterness, anger, and rejection. She felt unloved, ugly, embarrassed, not worthy, and like a failure. She feared never being loved again. Now, after calling on her superhero mindset and moving forward with new purpose, her new beliefs focus on living a life of giving. She has a never-give-up mentality and believes she is worthy, a true overcomer.

Simone is now a health and wellness coach living in South Africa. She is giving back, and her passion is to help as many people as she can by sharing her story so others can see hope. Simone believes that mindset is powerful, and everyone should call on their superhero mindset to get through difficult times.

Understanding Your Own Journey

The path is much closer than you expect. My hope is that you are now aware and have made the decisive decision to change the way you handle the adversity. In doing so, you will find it no longer owns you. Your adversity will no longer limit you or prevent your inevitable growth and evolution. Not today, not a chance. However, you have to take control over your journey and craft the path ahead if you want to continue to grow. It sometimes must be forged by fire, other times through thoughtful and strategic steps that move you in the direction of overcoming your limiting beliefs.

ROB SWYMER

One story comes to mind. On January 15, 2009, US Airways Flight 1549, an Airbus A320 on a flight from New York City's LaGuardia Airport to Charlotte, North Carolina, struck a flock of birds shortly after take-off, losing all engine power. Unable to reach any airport for an emergency landing, pilots Chesley "Sully" Sullenberger and Jeffrey Skiles glided the plane to a ditching in the Hudson River off Midtown Manhattan. All 155 souls on board were rescued by nearby boats, with few serious injuries. In a steady voice, Sullenberger issued a stern warning to passengers: "This is the captain. Brace for impact." I had the pleasure of seeing Sully speak at one of my company kickoffs. He recounted those now famous words. As I watched him speak, it was no surprise that he did exactly what he was supposed to do and that he was the right person to be in the captain seat that day. Even as he recounted the story of that day, his voice, body language, and overall presence was calm and reassuring.

This water landing became known as the "Miracle on the Hudson." Through the actions of the pilots, 155 souls were saved. As I listened to passenger interviews, I saw a pattern. They all had a reason to move forward and take action. The desire was strong enough and their pain was substantial enough that the only alternative to inevitable death was action. Maybe it was a wife wanting to get home for her husband or a grandmother determined to see her grandchild again, but in every case, these passengers found a way to surrender to what was happening and move forward with purpose. They didn't collapse under the stress but did what they had to do to get off the plane to safety.

I read the stories of those who stepped up. Passengers carried babies to safety, barked out orders to others to get

94

them moving off the plane, and calmed those who might have been in shock. During an interview, one passenger said, "I was excited to be part of this experience." Really? The passenger was excited to be part of a near-death experience? That is what we call embracing adversity and dealing with it. He found a solution and moved forward. We can all take this as a lesson, no matter your adversity.

I am sure you can overcome whatever you face—if you decide to do so. But you should make the decision to face your adversity and cast aside the limiting beliefs that hold you back. Change your inner voice, change your life.

Here is a simple exercise you can do to overcome your limiting beliefs. Ask yourself the following question: If your best friend had the same limiting belief, what would you tell him or her? How would you respond if your friend said, "I am just not smart enough for that" or "I don't have the right skills to do that"? We know the answer. And if that's the case, why can't you say the same thing to yourself? Our inner voice is more powerful than any outside voice we hear. The inner voice is cunning and manipulative and can sell you anything. You need to be on guard and ready to conquer that voice.

Enjoying the Journey of Others

Cheryl Hunter was traveling abroad as a teenager when she was kidnapped for trafficking by two criminals who held her captive, tortured her, and eventually left her for dead. Cheryl survived this life-changing trauma and now uses her experience to help people rise after facing adversity. She has written two best-selling books on overcoming adversity. In her research, she wanted to identify why some people come back from adversity and others do not.

She discovered the key was not to allow yourself to be held captive by your adversity. To me, this is all about the story we tell ourselves. If you let your adversity define who you are, then you will always be the victim. But if you change your inner voice or, as Cheryl says, "crack the code on your adversity," then you can move through the tragedy to thrive again.

Even though you may not be able to relate to the details of her story, we all, at some point in our life, need to overcome adversity. Cheryl talks about the two Cs as a means to do this: connection and charge. First, you must make a connection with someone who matters. This is what I talk about when I recommend serving and building connections with others. This is all part of the self-care process. She also talks about charging your batteries, which is doing what you love and are passionate about to solidify your purpose. The two Cs center around contribution, serving others, and self-care.

Or consider the story of Kris Carr, a thirty-two-year-old New Yorker who went to a regular checkup at her doctor's office and ended up diagnosed with a rare and incurable stage IV cancer called epithelioid hemangioendothelioma. She could have succumbed to the disease, and no one would have judged her, given the diagnosis. Instead, she decided to fight with all her will. She attacked her cancer with a nutritional lifestyle and turned her experience into a series of successful self-help books and documentaries. Today, Kris has her own wellness website, is a *New York Times* best-selling author, and is revered as one of the most prominent experts on healthy living. She did not give up, but she did give in, which gave her the ability to pivot and move forward with new purpose and perspective. Kris considers herself a cancer thriver, not just a survivor.

We create empowerment by understanding our own journey and by enjoying the journey of others. From others' testimonies, we draw motivation, inspiration, and excitement to forge ahead. We can learn from their stories if we do more than just read them. Take the lessons of each story and how they overcame adversity and apply those principles to your life.

Empowerment Is Everywhere

Now that we have acknowledged the presence of our own limiting beliefs and worked to turn down the volume on those messages while also drawing inspiration from others, we can craft a life filled with empowerment. Empowerment is everywhere. But it is up to each of us to create a path of empowerment. It does not come easily. In the end, it is up to you. Empowering beliefs are like gas for the engine, fueling you and moving you to great success. Though you have recognized and silenced your limiting beliefs, that is not enough. Now, more than ever, you need to call on your superhero mindset and create a new vision for yourself.

I believe that the solution to handling the adversity in our life is to focus on progress, if you can make even a bit of progress on a regular basis, then you feel alive. This gives us permission not to put pressure on ourselves for a specific outcome. If we focus on the process and take little steps forward, all will be good.

In his international bestseller *Atomic Habits*, James Clear discusses this principle: "It is easy to get bogged down trying to find the optimal plan for change: the fastest way to lose weight, the best program to build muscle, the perfect idea for a side hustle. We are so focused on figuring out the

best approach that we never get around to taking action."
As Voltaire said, "The best is the enemy of the good." I tell
people all the time about the two-millimeter rule. Make
small changes, and you will get massive results.

You don't have to be perfect; you just have to show progress. The need for perfection has killed more big ideas
than you can imagine. The key is to keep trying, keep moving forward, and keep pivoting to your new purpose and
perspective. When I was beginning my journey toward sobriety, I would have absolutely given up had I focused on
getting twenty-seven years of sobriety on the first day. But
putting twenty-four hours together at a time was something I could handle. We have a joke in AA: when you are
struggling, just say, "I will drink tomorrow." Of course,
tomorrow brings another day and another twenty-four-
hour opportunity to fight for sobriety. Take what you relate to from mine and other stories you have heard so far
and remember that it is your journey and only yours.

To recap, here are key strategies for overcoming adversity and creating change in your life.

1. **Have a plan.** A plan sets your vision for
   where you want to go and how you will
   get there. It includes the steps you are
   going to take, the tools you will use, and
   the outcome you will achieve in the end. It
   should also include the people who will
   help you make this plan come to life.
2. **Take action.** At first, "action" could be
   simple changes in your behavior, your
   outlook, and your state of mind. The key is
   to move forward, however small the step

may be. Moving forward is always better than standing still.

3. **Accept grace.** I have already talked about some of my God moments, but you should open your heart to receiving yours. Give yourself permission to be vulnerable and open to what the universe will send you.

4. **Be stronger than excuses.** Success is 80 percent mindset and only 20 percent strategy. Stop believing the excuses and forge ahead.

5. **Give 100 percent.** It is important to show up—all the time and with all your effort. That means you are mentally and physically present in all you do, whether you are attending a meeting with your team or your child's soccer game. They say a marriage is a 50/50 proposition. I say it is 100/100. Both participants need to enter the relationship to give and not get.

6. **Be comfortable being uncomfortable.** Adopting a growth mindset will mean learning to tolerate the distress that comes with change.

7. **Move forward.** Decide your destiny and build momentum.

8. **Break limiting beliefs.** Your beliefs form your reality. Break through your limiting beliefs and create new, powerful beliefs and goals.

9. **Be a creator.** Be an active creator of your life, not a victim of circumstances.

10. **Surrender to your new purpose and perspective.** Get out of yourself; get a mentor; start to give back.

Remember, your journey is your own. This chapter should empower you to create a path to overcome your limiting beliefs. We all have those voices in our head that interfere with our growth and progress. But as we increase our awareness of their impact, we can change the script. As the architects of the outcome, we are then empowered to see the world in a remarkable light and for exactly what it is: a place of endless opportunity.

chapter 8

Growing Pains: Surrender to Grow Bigger and Stronger

The words you attach to your experience become your experience.

—Tony Robbins

T ony Robbins has made one point very clear every time I have been in his presence: "The words you attach to your experience become your experience." *Webster's Dictionary* defines the ability to surrender as "continuing to take action as opposed to just giving up." Giving up—a very different concept than surrender—is defined as quitting a habit or withdrawing from something. Giving in or surrendering is letting something happen or giving way for something new to happen. This is why the simple, yet important act of surrender is the first step toward finding your new purpose, the first step toward moving on and thriving again. Think of the old joke, "AA is for quitters." Of course, that couldn't be

101

further from the truth. The real healing in AA starts when you surrender, when you are humbled, when your heart is opened to accepting something new, a new purpose.

The goal is to reach a place where you are moving toward healing. In the hurricane of pain, you are leaning into it, rather than constantly avoiding, fighting, and disregarding it. Do that and you will find gratitude in the journey. This is an infinite process that you should work on over the course of your lifetime. This is not a one-and-done undertaking. Each lesson learned is applied to the next adversity faced. You build your resilience muscle each time, just like going to the gym and building body muscle.

Quitting and surrendering are two very different things. The most important difference is that quitting is final, with no further action to move forward. In stark contrast, when you surrender, you take action to move in a different direction, a different path. When I was getting sober, I would say that I quit drinking. But in my new purpose, I was surrendering to the reality that I could not drink like everyone else. My body reacts differently to alcohol. Because of that, I needed to stop drinking. The definition of quitting for me would have been to continue drinking, allowing the world around me to simply collapse.

Instead, by surrendering, I was able to change my inner voice, create a new path for myself, and live and thrive without alcohol in my life. The real healing didn't start until I did that. In fact, I was sobor over a year before I was able to surrender and give in. I was what you call a "dry drunk," meaning I did not drink but I also did not work the program. I did not surrender and give in to the reality that I couldn't drink again and that I need help to get better.

Admitting you have failed is difficult for most people. No matter who you are or your walk of life, we all have a hard time dealing with failure or quitting. So, I ask you not to utter the word *quit*. Let's turn it to a positive: *surrender*. We know that surrender starts you on the path to change through dedicated action. In the end, there is no such thing as failing, there are just outcomes.

Quitting Is a Mindset

It is all about mindset, how you approach a situation. For example, when I look back at my adversity, I know that I learned from each experience and would not be who I am without these events. You should work to lean into the adversity or challenge you are facing to conquer it, overcome it, and learn from it. I would not be the person I am today if I hadn't gone through those life events. The truth is, there are no shortcuts. I love this saying: "If you walk in the woods for two hours, it will probably take two hours to come back out of the woods."

Remember, quitting is to stop, cease, or discontinue. Isn't it just another way of saying, "I have endured enough pain and I am sick and tired of being sick and tired?" or "I have had enough, and it is time to rise up. I am not going to stay in this place for one second more." Pain creates emotion and emotion creates action.

But what about failing? I subscribe to the notion of failing fast, which means learning from that failure and then moving on with a different path to success. I was taught that if and when you fail, you must get up and try it another way. If you fail again, you get up and do it again, yet a different way. Winners do that until they are successful. Hall of Fame college basketball coach John

Wooden said, "Failure isn't fatal, but failure to change might be."[13]

Failure is just another muscle to develop. Yes, you lean into failure, you fail fast and pivot, and then you move on with new purpose each time until you get it right. The only real failure is when you stop trying. It all goes back to the triad I learned from my work with Tony Robbins and described in chapter two: focus, language, and physiology. Focus on the future, not the past; focus on the solution, not the problem. Change the language you are using both internally and externally. We do this through showing up with conviction and living in the moment. Tap into your superhero mindset and step up to your new purpose in life, your new story, your new perspective.

Michael Jordan, after being cut from his high school basketball team, went home, locked himself in his room, and cried. Oprah Winfrey was demoted from her job as a news anchor because she "wasn't fit for television." Walt Disney was fired from a newspaper job for "lacking imagination and having no original ideas." The Beatles were rejected by Decca Recording Studios who said, "We don't like their sound; they have no future in show business."[14] Can you imagine a world without any of these amazing individuals? What would our world be without Mickey? When I was in high school, I was told that I should focus my energy on a trade because I would never go to college. Your internal story is way more powerful than any external story. You need to create your future

---

[13] White, Janessa, "Failure is Good for You," September 11, 2017, https://softwareforgood.com/failure-is-good-for-you.

[14] Trotter, Phil, "Hooks," accessed July 18, 2021, https://softwareforgood.com/failure-is-good-for-you.

and be involved in your own rescue. After all, it is your future, isn't it?

The quitter mentality is one of finality. You think, *I have nowhere to go, nothing else to try. I have tried everything I can to overcome.* Have you really? Can you look yourself in the eye with conviction and tell yourself that story? Remember, don't be the victim; be the solution. I have heard thousands of stories where people have overcome massive odds. In every case, they changed the story they were telling themselves or the story they were told growing up. Good thing Tom Brady didn't listen to that story, now considered the greatest quarterback of all time—or the GOAT—he wasn't even considered for a college position at one point. If Tom had listened to the story of defeat, he would not be rewriting history in the NFL today. Winston Churchill's words come to mind: "Success is stumbling from failure to failure with no loss of enthusiasm."[15]

We can fail, or, as I like to say, fall forward with each new adversity, each new challenge, and grow. What if we looked at failure as a positive thing? What if we went toward it, celebrated it, and embraced what it taught us each time? Think about the unlimited potential you would enjoy if you just let go and accepted the fact that you could fail but it would be okay. The biggest regret you will have is that you didn't learn from your mistakes. With each failure, it is important to regroup and go in a different direction. This is when the change will happen. Learn from your past, but do not live there.

---

[15] https://www.goodreads.com/author/quotes/14033.Winston_S_Churchill.

Surrender Is the Journey That Doesn't End

The reality is you never complete the journey of surrender. As a popular sporting goods company reminds us, "There is no finish line." Life is a journey of continuous growth and learning. I learned from my most horrific life events: AA, losing my wife, dealing with depression, having thoughts of suicide, and facing a life of blindness. Yet I still work every day to keep moving forward. After almost thirty years of sobriety, I still attend meetings on a regular basis and read *The Big Book*. I reach out to other alcoholics and serve them. I still say the Serenity Prayer every day.

While I don't have thoughts of suicide anymore, I remember that feeling like it was yesterday. That memory reminds me to constantly work on myself and that living in a beautiful state is non-negotiable. That means living in a state of gratitude and reaching out for help as needed. Another great quote that I can bring to you is, "If you are in your head, you are dead."

You will find no greater investment than investing in yourself. This is why the journey never ends. You should always be working on yourself every day, always striving to get to the next level. I am so grateful for adversity because it made me stronger. Each setback, each life event, no matter how small, prepares me for the next one. The key is to use those events to your advantage. Lean in and embrace adversity; do not fear it.

One way to learn from failure is to turn it into a positive. Sarah Blakely, CEO of Spanx, once said, "The definition of failure is not about the outcome, but about not trying."[16]

---

[16] Segal, Gillian Zoe, "This Self-Made Billionaire Failed the LSAT Twice, then Sold Fax Machines for 7 Years Before Hitting Big—Here's

You only fail if you don't try. The benefit of a crisis or pain is that it makes us try new things and then lean into them. When we see a compelling future, then we can come up with the pathway to success. It is a known fact that our thoughts and feelings have an electromagnetic reality, so manifest wisely. What you put in the universe is important. James Lane Allen said, "Adversity does not build character, it reveals it."[17] What does your character look like? Are you satisfied with it? Are there areas you would like to improve?

Some experience life with very little or no adversity, failure, or challenge. Then, somewhere along the line, they experience a setback. Unfortunately, they have not built up the muscle needed. This is like the natural athlete who excels in the game and doesn't need to practice; that luck will only take him so far. Life eventually throws curve balls, and you have to practice to be ready. So, be grateful for your adversity, your failures, and your setbacks. Simply put, no adversity, no growth.

It is so important to continue to work on yourself, whatever that means to you. Maybe you read self-help books or attend seminars to learn new principles to apply to your life. In the same way we build habits for your physical health, it is all about being consistent. If you are trying to get healthy or build muscle, the key is consistency. If you even go to the gym on days you don't feel up to it, then you will grow. It is the same with your mental state. Do something every day to better yourself mentally, raise

How She Got There," April 3, 2019, https://www.cnbc.com/2019/04/03/self-made-billionaire-spanx-founder-sara-blakely-sold-fax-machines-before-making-it-big.html.
[17] Unknown Author, "Crisis and Leadership," accessed July 18, 2021, https://fedcapgroup.org/crisis-and-leadership.

your game, and get to a peak state. This might be meditation or mindfulness exercises. You might listen to motivational podcasts each day or write in your gratitude journal. Every action is a step toward gaining momentum, and as we know, momentum is the key to moving forward and growing.

The Path to Surrender Goes through Brick Walls

As I dove into what a person goes through when facing adversity, especially a life-altering event, I saw six distinct phases you should try to push through. The first five are the stages of grief made popular by Elisabeth Kubler Ross's research. In my research for this book, I conducted interviews with people from all walks of life who had faced different adversity and saw that these are, indeed, universal phases of the experience:

1. Denial: You refuse to believe something is happening or happened.
2. Anger: Once you believe, you become angry that it happened or that you let it happen.
3. Bargaining: You negotiate with yourself for false hope that you can force a change.
4. Depression: You become hopeless, essentially giving up.
5. Acceptance: You surrender; this is the turning point that allows you to give in and pivot to a new purpose.
6. Action: You can now put your plan into place and change your path.

Now, most people struggle through each of these, often getting stuck in the phases of denial, anger, and depression—never getting to surrender. It takes a great deal of time to fully accept what has occurred. The faster you get through denial and anger and move to surrender, the faster you can get to a place of growth. Surrender is where we grow and overcome the pain in our lives. It should be our greatest goal to put in the work and understand that the first three phases will only have as much impact as we allow them to. If we change the paradigm of going through these phases, we reduce the suffering and increase our ability to learn and build resilience more quickly. Let's take each phase and break it down.

Denial. Oh, how easy it is to deny that anything is happening and bury our head in the sand. We think, *If I just deny it's there, it will go away.* How crazy does that sound? How many times do we just wish the problem away and not face it? We tell ourselves that it is either not real or that it will take care of itself in time with no action required. In my case, I denied that I had a drinking problem for over a decade and justified my actions based on the story I was telling myself. "I am in sales, and I need to go out and drink with clients to help build connections." Now that I am sober for close to thirty years, I realize how that story was not healthy or real.

Anger. Anger is resentment turned upside down. And resentment is not worth the effort. Why hold anger or resentment toward someone or something and hurt yourself along the way? As Nelson Mandela once said, "It is like taking poison and hoping it will kill your enemies."[18]

---

[18] https://www.goodreads.com/quotes/144557-resentment-is-like-drinking-poison-and-then-hoping-it-will.

Anger holds you hostage and keeps you from growing, so get rid of it. Stay in a healthy state of mind and you will accelerate through this phase of adversity.

Bargaining. We next decide that we can negotiate our way out of the problem. When I was drinking and wanted to deny I had a problem, I would say, "I will just drink wine, or I will drink only on the weekends." I would negotiate with myself instead of facing that I had a problem. Some bargain with God when in adversity, making promises to change their life if he will remove the obstacle.

Depression. When bargaining does not work, we sink into the next phase: depression. If we are not careful, we will get comfortable in this phase and eventually give up. Only you can change your inner voice and get out of this phase. This is also when you need to reach out to professionals who have the skill set to help you overcome the feelings of hopelessness to get to the next phase.

Acceptance. As you struggle and suffer through denial, anger, bargaining, and depression, the hope is to eventually reach a pivotal point in your journey: acceptance. During this phase, you accept adversity and embrace the learning experience. Navy SEALs, the most elite military unit of the US Armed Forces, has a saying, "Embrace the suck." It is their way of saying that there will be adversity, so embrace it, be grateful for it, and learn from it. This philosophy mirrors Buddhist teachings. When we deny what reality is giving us, what is really happening, then we create suffering. And it is only suffering if we label it so. Your experiences are based on the language you use and the label you put on each of them. By embracing them and even thanking them, you will see them as a positive learning experience that will take you to a new level. When you accept adversity, you can then visualize a path to your new purpose, which brings you to your next and final phase.

Action. Action is the final and most powerful phase of overcoming adversity. It is in the action that we see measurable progress, momentum, and change. Action means courageously moving ahead, knowing you are going in the right direction. Remember the two-millimeter rule? The smallest changes can yield the biggest results. Small steps forward can help you gain the momentum needed for true change. But it starts with your mindset; you should try to get that right first. Then you can show up to change, show up to think differently, and show up to move forward with new purpose.

I remember when I was first getting sober. The most important thing I needed to do was attend meetings. I was told the key to my development would be to attend an AA meeting once a day for a minimum of ninety consecutive days. That one step helped me gain momentum for working the program and staying sober to this day.

Everywhere we look, there are examples of people fighting through adversity. Just consider my friend Jessica Kate. She is a true example of overcoming extreme challenges to develop strength and independence from a young age. I think of her as a self-improvement powerhouse. When Jessica was a little girl, her family didn't have much, and her parents were barely adults themselves. Although they didn't have much in way of material possessions, they lived an extraordinary life up in the mountains away from society. They didn't have a farm, but they did have animals. She was raised with more than your average dog as a pet. They had small quantities, yet a variety of chickens, goats, sheep, cows, ducks, and a carpet snake named Slippery. On winter mornings, Jessica would run down to the chook pen in her cozy dressing gown and warm slippers, and collect the tiny bantams, wrapping them in the pockets of her dressing gown to keep them warm. Jessica and her sister would then sit on the trampoline with the bantams, patting their heads and giggling at the little sounds they would make, expressing their gratitude for keeping them warm while they watched the sunrise. Surrounded by nature, Jessica witnessed the circle of life on a daily basis. David Attenborough was of regular entertainment in her home too when her dad wasn't playing his guitar and singing out loud. Life was anything but ordinary . . . until it was.

Fast forward to Jessica as a grown woman in her twenties working a corporate job in a law firm, putting in ten-hour days and struggling to get ahead as she paid off her car loan and prepared to start her own business on the side. Gone were the days of appreciating nature or sunrises. In her thirties, she got married, bought her dream home, dream car, and her business was thriving. Jessica was now putting in twelve-hour days, six days a week. Her staff stressed her out and she barely had time to connect with her husband or have a social life. Jessica didn't take the time to stop and appreciate what she had. She only knew how to keep moving forward and focus on what was next. Gone were the days of appreciating anything, certainly not herself or her time.

Then . . . the unimaginable happened. Jessica received a phone call that changed her life forever. Her dearest father had decided to take his own life and leave this world—the world that she had let consume her. The world that she had failed to stop and appreciate for what it's worth. The world that no longer made sense to Jessica. Suddenly, everything she had sacrificed herself for seemed pointless.

Everything she thought that mattered, didn't. Every material item she owned seemed worthless. You see, somewhere between watching sunrises on the farm and working a corporate job in her twenties, life turned *ugly*.

Jessica's parents fought terribly, and throughout their war of domestic violence and drug abuse, Jessica went into survival mode. Leaving home at seventeen to fend for herself, she lost all sense of the meaning of "being." Jessica fell victim to the idea of "doing" what she thought would make her happy, instead of "being" *who* would make her happy.

The truth is, Jessica had no idea who she really wanted to be. She just created an identity of the person she thought she needed to be in order to survive and achieve all the "doing." And so, she had to learn how to start over. She had to learn how to press reset and practice "being" all over again. This proved to be more difficult than she thought. Jessica had to learn to surrender and break free from her survival mode, to undo years of subconscious programming that put her in that survival mode. She found it confronting and uncomfortable at times. She resisted and put up a good fight, until she realized she was only at war with herself.

Today, life is different for Jessica. She not only takes the time to appreciate those sunrises and sunsets, but she thrives in the essence of "being." Every moment she chooses to be present and appreciate just being, Jessica reflects and learns from her former self. It's her way of honoring that little girl on the trampoline that didn't know how to make sense of the world, but learned how precious it is — to just simply *be*. As an international success mindset coach, Jessica is now a voice for empowerment. She is the founder and CEO of Inspiring Minds Movement, which is a global community of people wanting to connect, learn, and grow, while creating the ultimate success for themselves, in life and business. This movement has the ultimate vision to share the relatable tools to make personal growth, success, and happiness attainable for everyone.

Although Jessica is a successful entrepreneur and a powerful inspirational speaker, she prefers to be known as a thought leader—educating, supporting, and inspiring everyone around the world to fulfil their passion and purpose. She has become a game-changer in the industry, guiding people to connect with their higher self—or, as I would say, their superhero mindset. She encourages people to acknowledge their worth and design a life they desire with absolute confidence.

Like Jessica Kate teaches us, the most important thing needed for action is a place to go. Where do you want your action to take you? For example, what is your life going to be once you begin to act and succeed? What will your new life look like? Visualize this new, amazing life. Where will you be after you move forward and conquer this adversity? Who will you be with? I always make it a point to visualize what my best life will look like in the future. So, I ask you to start now, however small a step. Moving forward, even a little bit, is better than going backward or, worse yet, standing still.

Bigger and Stronger

As I have said, growth comes with surrender and action. There is no better feeling than being dedicated to growth and a cause that is bigger than you. For many, it can take days, weeks, even months or years to get to a point of surrender/action. When you overcome your adversity and move through these phases, you become bigger and stronger. You have built up your resilience muscle and are able to navigate and withstand all the pain and suffering life has sent your way. More important, you will be able to handle the next setback that will inevitably come your way.

Youth Poet Amanda Gorman, who spoke at President Biden's inauguration in 2021, said it well: "Just *if* versus just *is* . . . not what *was* but what *shall be*."[19] This sums up what we need to do to change our story. Language has power, especially the language we use inside ourselves.

After not working the program for over a year and staying in what I call the never-ending circle of resentment, I finally surrendered, and life completely changed for me. It was in that moment that I learned to love the moments. I realized that life was happening *for* me and not *to* me. I had a clear picture of where I wanted to go and how I could get there. As I got stronger in my convictions, I was able to get out of myself and help others.

That is when the real growth happened. When you turn outward and come from a place of giving rather than getting, the universe rewards you with something called gratitude. This is the foundation of living in a beautiful state for me and something I take very seriously. No matter how bad things got for me while I was going through any of my life events, I could always find something to be grateful for. This is a mindset shift and is the most important way to build the foundation of a better life, a life worth living.

Now that you have spent time building your resilience muscle, it is important to keep working at it and never go

---

[19] Gorman, Amanda, "The Hill We Climb: the Amanda Gorman Poem that Stole the Inauguration Show," January 20, 2021, https://www.theguardian.com/us-news/2021/jan/20/amanda-gorman-poem-biden-inauguration-transcript.

back to where you came from. Unused muscles experience atrophy. If you spend months losing weight and you then gain it all back, a damaging and often devastating cycle begins to unfold in your mind. If you are going to put the time into growth and massive change, make it count, make it last. Always look for the next level you can get to, the next life event that needs conquering. Adopt a growth mindset for your life and your future, and it will serve you well.

When you find yourself in the unfamiliar territory of loss, embrace it, lean into it, and learn from it. You are dealing with a failed relationship? Good. Dealing with a difficult boss at work? Good. Dealing with a health issue? Good. This is an opportunity to embrace, accept, and surrender so you can pivot and take action and grow from the pain. I am like a sponge when it comes to learning and applying new principles. I love learning new techniques that enable me to go to the next level. Even more important is taking those around me to that level as well.

chapter 9

Live and Thrive: The Roadmap to Find Your Purpose

The moment of surrender is not when life is over.
It's when it begins.

—Marianne Williamson

I t's all between your ears. It has taken me years upon years of pain, suffering, growth, and development to understand the tremendous value of that simple yet powerful statement. A paradigm shift is a remarkable transformation in your mindset as it relates to how you view a challenge, situation, or experience. It is like exchanging blindness for the ability to see clearly, to focus, and to understand that which stands in front of you.

The truth is, I never understood what this all meant until I worked on myself and peeled back the layers of my belief system. It was only then that I truly realized I had the power to change the way I perceived myself. I learned that I alone could change my mindset, no matter how low I might be or how much pain I am experiencing. Changing perception is a superpower of sorts. Inevitably, it led to my superhero mindset. I know without a doubt that if I am in a room full of one hundred people, I have an advantage over everyone. I can put myself in the right mindset, the right state, in a snap of my finger. It is an acquired skill, but one of which I am very proud. But you have to make a choice to do the work. You should remain dedicated to learning how and practice it along the way. Progress rather than perfection, as the program taught me, is what I strive for, what I celebrate, and what I live for.

The Superhero Mindset Superpower

Shifting your mindset is your superpower. It is what sets you apart from anyone else in the world that is going through adversity or dealing with a challenging event. What I have learned from everything I have gone through is that mindset is a very powerful thing. Just like your favorite superhero, you need to learn how to harness that power and use it to your advantage. There are many ways you can influence or even change your mindset, but here are a few things I use to help me when I need to make the shift:

1. **Learn to meditate.** Meditation is the best way to ground yourself and learn to be present. Sometimes the best action plan is to take no action but to be still and in the moment. Mindfulness meditation is known as the practice of nonjudgmental,

intentional awareness of the present. It can strengthen areas of your brain responsible for memory, learning, attention, and self-awareness. This practice can also help calm the sympathetic branch of your nervous system, putting you in a parasympathetic state, which allows clear thinking, reduces stress, and gives you more focus.

2. **Make personal development a priority.** Always be learning and growing. Seek out experts, books, podcast, and Ted Talks. Surround yourself with those that you can learn from. Those that will take you to the next level. Embrace the growth mindset of continuous learning every day. Seek out knowledge and never stop grabbing all you can learn. And learn with an open mind where anything is possible.

3. **Live each day in gratitude.** Be grateful for the little things in life as much as you are for the big ones. Be grateful for the warm breeze or the sunshine just as much as the house you call home.

4. **Focus on your long-term vision.** Only you have the power to create your destiny, and that begins with a clear vision for yourself. Remember that most people underestimate what they can do in five years and overestimate what they can do in two. Set big dreams and manifest the vision you want for yourself.

5. **Listen to trusted advisors and mentors.**
Ask for help. There is a remarkable
amount of people who are willing to guide
you and mentor you along your way.
Many of them have walked the walk and
have tons of lessons to impart upon you
that will assist you in moving forward in a
meaningful way. Seek them out and ask
for help and guidance.

6. **Practice vulnerability.** Make yourself
vulnerable to others; build trust and
human connections. Don't be afraid to
show your vulnerability or fail. The
learning is in the loss, not the win. We
celebrate the wins; we learn from the
losses. You need to put that into perspective and spend more time on the fails so
you can learn from them and move on
quickly. There is no growth without
vulnerability.

7. **Push yourself.** In pursuing growth
through my discomfort, one of the ways I
faced my fears was to walk over fire. I can
tell you that when you walk over sixteen-
hundred-degree hot coals, you feel like
you can face anything without fear. I did it
to work on my limiting beliefs, to better
understand where they came from. Once I
did that, I shattered false beliefs and lived
without any limits at all. It comes down to
your mindset and the story you tell
yourself. That is just one way I pushed
myself.

Your mindset has the power to change anything. When you change your inner voice, you can live in faith and not fear. Part of living in faith is letting go of what you cannot control and turning it over to a higher power. Living in faith opens us up to the universe to accept what comes our way. As I mentioned, you must be aware of and accept the God moments that come your way.

At times during the COVID lockdown, I have joked that it seems like we are in an expensive prison here in London. With nowhere to go, it would be easy to spiral downward. For me, the choice to live in faith, not fear, is what keeps me going. It keeps me in a positive mindset and enables me to share that vision with everyone I connect. These days, that means those I see on video calls.

In the end, the story you tell yourself and what you believe is possible will shape your future. I choose to make living in a beautiful state non-negotiable, and I pass that philosophy on to anyone I can. Even in the darkest of hours, when I am struggling or in a down mood, I look for ways to get out of myself and serve others. This could be giving back to the community or mentoring someone. It could be as simple as giving someone a smile on the street as you pass by. I believe you can always find something to be grateful for. For example, the parks in London are open, and what beauty they offer. I never took the time to look at nature and its beauty before. This time of forced social distancing gave me new perspective, a new vision of the world around me.

It has been said that this time during the pandemic is a reset of sorts, a reset for the planet, our environment, for humanity. I believe that is true to an extent. I feel that I have reset and evaluated what is important to me, who is important to me. Material things have taken a back seat and relationships and connection with others have become a priority. Human connections are made virtually now but are still as strong. When we see a neighbor on the front stoop, we wave more often; we say hello and smile.

I am not sure what normal will look like when this all passes, and it will. But the truth is, we ultimately get to create our destiny by creating a vision for our future. Will we go back to normal and bury ourselves in our phones, or will we be present and mindful? Will we spend more time at home with family and friends and less time chasing the next event or milestone? Only time will tell, but I like to think that this reset will not only get us ready for the new normal, but it will also enable us to accelerate through it with new perspective and purpose. If we go back to the way it was, we will have learned nothing.

No matter your intentions or physical abilities, your mind should fully buy in and commit to the process to complete the shift. I once heard a story of a dad who would celebrate when his children failed, even more than when they succeeded. The message was simple; he believed you learn more from your failure than your success.

One of the greatest takeaways of this book is that the more adversity one has in their life, the stronger and more resilient they become. The triad of influence Tony Robbins teaches allows us to change your state and create your destiny. But I also use it to change my inner voice and the story I am telling myself.

Language. Think of the three sides of a triangle like this: first, language. What story are we telling ourselves and what limiting belief is getting in the way of thriving again after adversity? If we begin to tell ourselves a different story, we can begin to change how we live our lives. How we talk to ourselves makes all the difference in the world.

For example, if our inner voice is negative, then we will gravitate toward the negative.

In that instance, we become a magnet for the negative. The people, places, and things in our life will reflect that orientation. A negative world could then become our comfort zone. But if the language we speak to ourselves is uplifting, positive, and forward thinking, we will attract the positive. Think of yourself as a magnet. What do you want to attract? What kind of people do you want to be attached to? What influences do you want to be surrounded by? Once you start attracting the right people, places, and things, more will follow in abundance.

Focus. Focus is the second axis. Are we focusing on the positive or the negative, the past or the future? When we speak to ourselves, is our focus on what we do not have or what we have? Do we show our gratitude every day for what we have? Do we focus on moving forward or giving up? I am a firm believer that my energy will go to whatever I focus on. Thus, I go there with conviction. It's a philosophy that I try and live by every single day. I want to focus on the most positive, forward-thinking actions I can because I know that is where my energy will come from. And when you are dealing with adversity that can pull you down, you will need energy to rise up. So, create energy by focusing on what you need to do, what action you need to take, and what future you want to live.

Physiology. How do we manifest our superhero mindset in our bodies? Do we lean in and own it with conviction and purpose, or are we timid and apprehensive? You see, the mind is where it all begins. Bring the mind, and all else will follow. And since we still have version 1.0 of our brain, we need to hack it and rewire it so we can thrive again and continue to overcome adversity.

One way to do that is to become a true superhero. Walk the walk and talk the talk. Move with purpose and conviction. I do not mean for you to be verbose or cocky. I mean you must move with both humility and swagger. You need to have the "I got this" mentality and believe that nothing is going to stop you from living your best life, nothing is going to get in the way of you thriving again, even after a huge life event. The "I got this" mindset will enable you to show up and be present for yourself. Then and only then can you manifest your future destiny and thrive. By making this move, you will also have this tool to use anytime you need it in the future.

It takes a growth mindset to accomplish this. Those with a growth mindset believe that these abilities can be developed and strengthened by way of commitment and hard work. It comes down to doing the work. Having a growth mindset is important because it can help you overcome any adversity you may face.[20] Growth mindsets understand the importance of persistence and determination. By changing the way you think, you can change the way you learn and adapt.

If you truly want to change your mindset and learn how to rewire your ten-thousand-year-old brain, you can. Become a lifelong learner and, above all, do not let your failures define you; let them motivate you and make you stronger.

Rubber Meets Road

We all should work to find our purpose and create our journey. The only way to do that is through crafting a

---

[20] Miller, Kori D., "5+ Ways to Develop a Growth Mindset Using Grit and Resilience," March 22, 2021, https://positivepsychology.com/5-ways-develop-grit-resilience.

roadmap to live and thrive by. It doesn't always come easily. For me, I found that it has to be a thoughtful and strategic movement.

As we come to the end of our time together, let's reflect on what we've learned. First, adversity builds resilience, and all adversity is a learning opportunity, even small life events. Arnold Schwarzenegger once said, "Strength does not come from winning; your struggles develop your strengths."[21]

Surrender is not giving up. Rather, it is giving in to your new purpose and new perspective. We then can move to the final phase, action. A good friend of mine, who is a retired special forces commander, put it like this, "When met with extreme opposition, you give in to your current position and regroup, formulate another plan, and attack with a new strategy." Even in war, surrender does not mean to give up.

Action is where we test and put into practice all we have learned. The most important thing to learn is that even the smallest steps forward will eventually contribute to gaining the momentum you need. Take time to recognize and celebrate the little wins just as much as the big ones. When someone tells me, they have done something positive for themselves, I always remind them to take a moment and celebrate that win. They usually give me a perplexed look and say something like, "It was just . . ." The truth is little moments add up and build resilience just as much as the larger life events.

Let's call it momentum stacking. In his book, *Atomic Habits*, James Clear discusses the concept of habit stacking, a process that involves grouping together small activities into a routine which you link to a habit already

---

[21] https://medium.com/@steveagyeibeyondlifestyle/strength-does-not-come-from-winning-28a369551737.

set in your day. This makes the routine memorable and anchors your new habits to an existing trigger. That is what we want to do with our small wins to build momentum toward a larger goal. I got the idea from the principles of AA. Here, we string together one day at a time. At the very beginning, it can even be one hour at a time. The point is you celebrate the positive actions you take.

Live and Thrive

In the final section of this chapter, we will detail and expand upon the following principles we have learned. This is the road map for you to use as you implement these changes into your life. Anyone can tap into their superhero mindset if they do the following:

1. **Use all life events, large or small, to build your resilience muscle.** This is where you can gain momentum by recognizing even the small events will stack together to prepare you for the larger life events.
2. **Surrender.** Before you can thrive again, you need to give in, not give up. Without this step, you will struggle and never get to your new purpose. The key here is to pivot and move forward in a new direction, one with new purpose and perspective.
3. **Ask for help.** Getting help is one of the most important aspects of building resilience, for no one can do it alone. Reach out to others for help, and in return, help others along the way. You will gain the trust of others and heal yourself at the same time.

4. **Accept that building resilience is an infinite journey.** Resilience isn't built in a day. So set your mind to be ready. You will conquer adversity and come out the other side stronger and wiser with a vision for your future.

5. **Develop a growth mindset.** Work on yourself all the time; never stop learning and growing. Stretch yourself to exceed your goals. Do in one year what you think you can do in two. Push yourself to break through limiting beliefs and go beyond your wildest dreams.

6. **Live a life of gratitude.** Make living in a beautiful state non-negotiable. Always start your day with a meditation or reflection that puts you in a state of gratitude. *Live* your life in the present— and in a *beautiful state*. Focus on what gives you the most joy and make that your life mission. When you do that, your real potential begins.

Parting Words

In Greek mythology, the centaur Chiron was a wounded healer after being poisoned with an incurable wound by one of Hercules's arrows. *Wounded healer* is a term credited to psychologist Carl Jung. The idea states that an analyst is compelled to treat patients because the analyst himself is "wounded." This concept is also true in AA. Only someone in the fellowship of AA can truly help another alcoholic. When facing any challenge or obstacle, it's best to have the help of someone who has gone before you.[22]

I wrote this book as a wounded healer. I hope I have given you the shortcuts, tools, and methods to get through whatever you might be facing. I am truly grateful for all I have been through. Without my trials, I would not be the person I am today. So, remember to embrace your adversity; after all, it is part of who you are. You are in this current moment because of all you have gone through. It is all right to acknowledge and accept where you are.

We have learned that surrender is the most important thing you can do when faced with adversity. My hope is that my story has proven that no matter what you go through, no matter how horrific it may be, you can not only survive but thrive once again. I am proof that the human spirit is strong and can survive anything with the right mindset.

I wish you a bright and amazing future. It has been my honor to serve you here and share a bit of what I have learned in my sixty years. Remember to keep learning and growing and working on yourself. It is the most important investment you can make. Do the work; take the risk; fail fast; and learn until the end. Above all, when faced with adversity in your life, surrender; give in and move forward with new purpose and perspective. If you do this, nothing will ever bring you down for good. Go find your superhero mindset and remember that the rise is always sweeter than the fall.

---

[22] Gerada, Clare, "The Wounded Healer—Why We need to Rethink How We Support Doctors," July 14, 2015, https://www.bmj.com/content/351/bmj.h3526.

acknowledgments

Through this process I have learned that if you want to really get out of your comfort zone, write a book. Even though this journey was one of the most challenging accomplishments of my life, I have enjoyed every second of it. I could not have accomplished this without the help of so many people along the way.

I want to thank Justin Spizman for keeping me on point and allowing me to tell my story in my own words.

In addition, I am so grateful for all those I met along this journey and to those that allowed me to share their stories within these pages, examples of true adversity and the ability to overcome and thrive again. A big thank you to:

Jabany Aguilar for his openness and vulnerability in sharing his story.

Gaelle Lebray for sharing her life lessons as she navigated life after divorce.

Jessica Kate for spending time with me to share her insights on how to thrive after adversity, give back and have a massive impact on others.

Sonia Singh for showing us that true grit will help you thrive again.

Russ Rausch for teaching me how to embrace my emotions and learn to "play nervous." To be present and focus on what you can control and let the rest go.

Tony Robbins and Tony Robbins Research for opening me up to so many new possibilities and allowing me to break through those limiting beliefs that were holding me back.

Simone Prinsloo for sharing her story of courage and how she not only survived cancer, but thrived after beating it.

Thank you to my AA fellowship, always there and never judging, the rock of my sobriety even after thirty years.

To my fellow authors that spent time with me, offered advice and encouragement to stay the course and be true to my vision for this project.

A big thank you to Lisa Earle McLeod for providing me with a great foreword and for her guidance and encouragement through this process.

To my children for encouraging me to share my story and give back. You have always loved me unconditionally. For that I am forever grateful.

Thank you to all those that have touched my life, some for just a moment, others for a lifetime. You are the reason that I have a story to tell and the reason I am here to tell it.